Hand Sewn by Machine

Marie Duncan & Betty Farrell

Krause Publications
700 E. State St.
Iola, WI 54990-0001
715-445-2214
www.krause.com

Please call or write for our free catalog of publications. Our toll-free number to place an order or obtain a free catalog is 800-258-0929 or please use our regular business telephone 715-445-2214 for editorial comment and further information.

Library of Congress Catalog Number 99-61454
ISBN 0-87341-799-2

Printed in the United States of America

Table of Contents

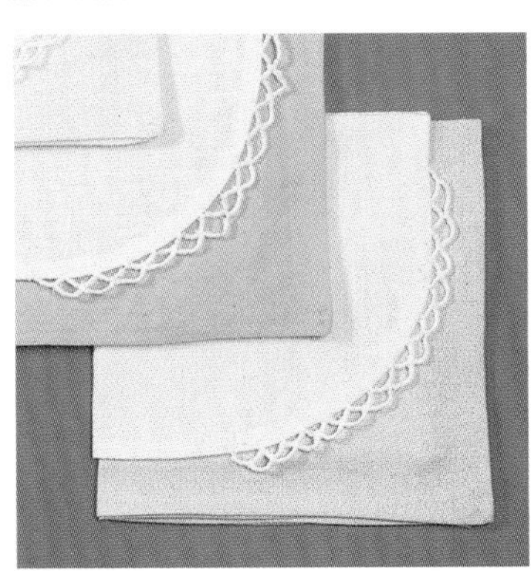

Introduction

"Hand sewing" brings forth the images of the beautiful heirloom treasures of past generations. This was an era when time was not at a premium, when women didn't juggle family, jobs, volunteer work, and husbands. They had time to spend creating a christening gown of the finest fabrics to be found, using the daintiest of laces and creating the perfect pintucks, practicing their embroidery until the stitches were perfectly even.

Embroidery, hand sewing, crocheting, and needlework were all taught to young girls, along with watercolor painting and piano lessons. These were talents highly treasured and admired in a young woman and passed on from their mothers and grandmothers.

Life today is often a saga of unfinished projects sitting in the drawers and of "ideas" floating around in our heads, ready to be stitched out, but becoming a victim of "not enough time!" How has our life changed? Spell check on the computer just tried to change "hand sewing," to "handgun." While poets continue to write poems that will survive the centuries in time, today they do it on their computer. Musicians hear the music in their head, as Mozart did centuries ago, but today it is recorded on CDs.

While we think we are unique in this aspect of our life, a book we ran across in our research, with a copyright date of 1936, states, "There may appear less time today than of yore, in which to produce works of elaborate nature; but there is always time to produce good small pieces."

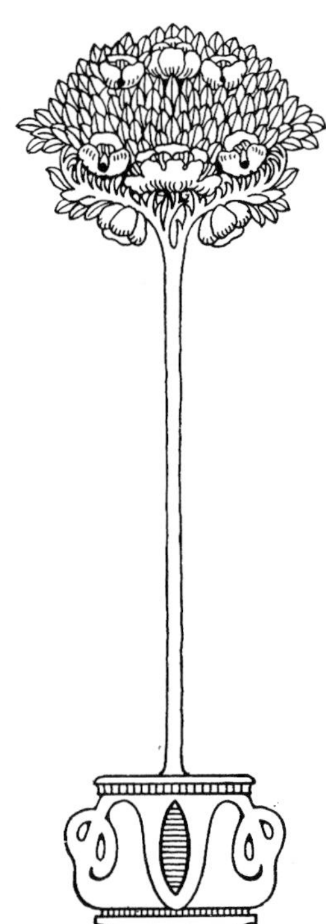

We offer to you, in *Hand Sewn by Machine*, the beauty, the magic, the creativity we all crave, in a manner you can duplicate and actually produce in a timely manner; now, today! We started with silk ribbon embroidery, always a hand technique that we brought to you, by machine, in *Ribbon Embroidery by Machine*, *More Ribbon Embroidery by Machine*, and *Celebrate the Seasons, with Ribbon Embroidery by Machine.*

Now we will expand into heirloom sewing, machine-made lace and crocheted lace, needlepoint, crewel embroidery, hardanger embroidery, Brazilian embroidery and more. All are done by machine. Most can be done on any zig zag sewing machine. We will still tell you occasionally to "do it by hand" if that is the best way. We want to offer the other "machine people" like us all possible machine techniques. What we won't do is sacrifice quality. Although we will require some special threads, fabrics, and needles, they are all readily available through your local fabric store or mail order sources we have given you.

Whether you start with the main project or the quick project to try out the technique, create now, enjoy and just say "thanks" to the many compliments that will come your way! Also keep your eyes and ears open to new ways to utilize your newly learned skills. Although we didn't have any brides in mind at this point in our lives, the re-embroidered lace we sewed on a child's dress collar would be an heirloom to be treasured forever in a bridal gown.

Materials and Terminology

This chapter is to familiarize you with some common materials, notions, threads, needles and terms relating to your sewing machine. We have tried to keep the majority of our projects such that they can be completed on fairly basic sewing machines. We will review the types of sewing machines needed for various projects and techniques, as well as assorted feet and accessories you might want to use to make the different techniques easier. We've divided it into these major areas: fabrics, notions, threads, needles, and sewing machines.

Fabrics:

When we call for a particular fabric such as linen, wool, cotton, etc., there is usually a reason relating to the particular technique we are doing. We try to give you alternatives, as many fabrics are not available in all areas of the country or they may not be suitable to your particular lifestyle.

Many of our techniques call for natural fibers, linen, cotton, and wool, because they will form, crease, or act like we want them to and retain that particular shape or texture. Man-made fibers, such as polyester, are created to resist wrinkles and forever retain the smooth crisp finish the factory applied. That is great in a blouse or shirt that you don't want to have to iron, but these fibers will fight you when you want them to fold over nicely and crease, and they have been taught to remain flat! While 100% linen is the best for many of our projects, it isn't worth two cents if it will sit in your drawer because you have no time to iron it. If this is you, instead try linen/cotton blend, linen-like fabrics with cotton and rayon, or cotton and poly. Your results will still be magnificent and the end product usable for your lifestyle. If you are in doubt, purchase 1/8-yard pieces of several fabrics and experiment.

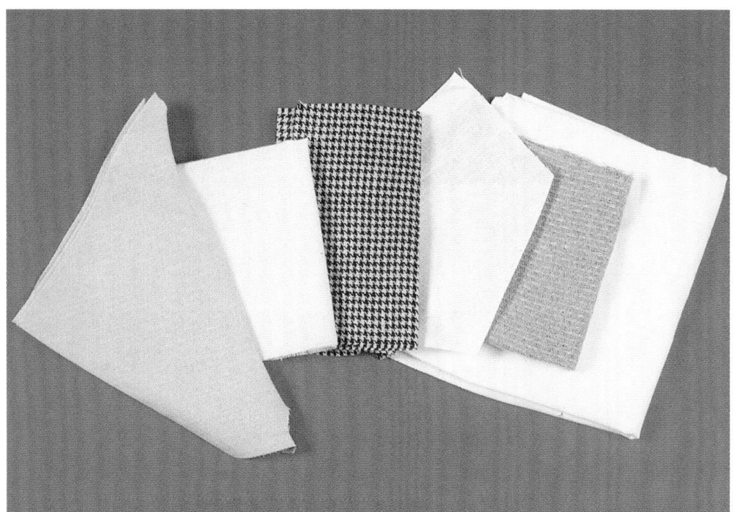

Notions:

Notions change on a daily basis and as this book goes to press, hundreds of new notions will be appearing in the marketplace. We mention some of our favorites, those which will make a given task easier, quicker, or sometimes just plain possible. If a particular notion is optional, we say that. If we say you NEED a particular item, trust us, you need it. For example, hemstitching cannot be done without a wing needle. Period.

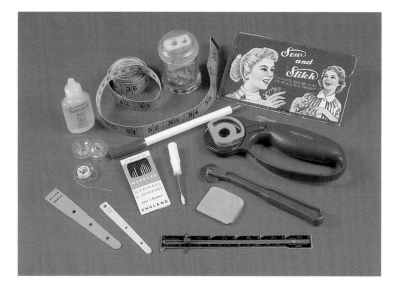

Stabilizers are a topic unto themselves, but we are including them in notions. A stabilizer is a base that is, for the most part, removed so as not to be a part of our finished stitching. They fall roughly into the following categories:

Water soluble: These can be like Solvy or Super Solvy by Sulky, which we use extensively with our laces and other projects because they are widely available and disappear completely. These are made from a gelatin-like substance originally created for hospitals to make laundry bags out of. These bags could be filled with contaminated articles of clothing or bedding and put directly into the washer, and then dissolve, eliminating the need for handling. There are other brand names available as well.

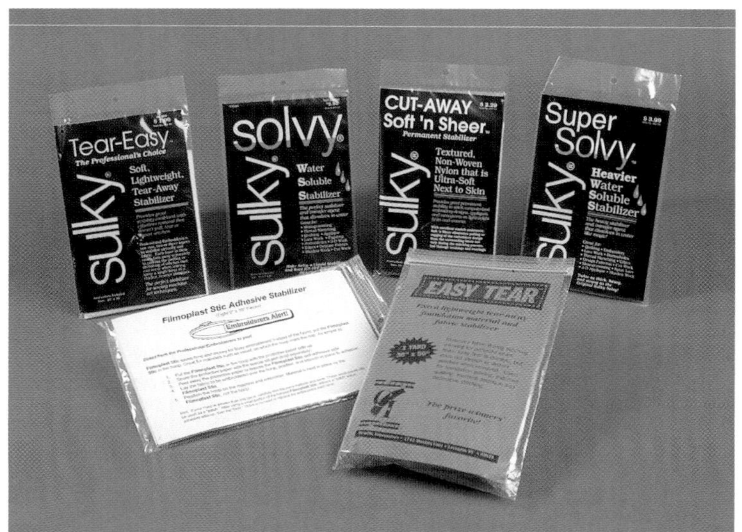

Tear away: These are used extensively under embroidery, as in the underside of an embroidered shirt. They are used on the inside of a garment, where the remaining "whiskers" won't matter. There are many different weights available under many different brand names.

Cut away: This is an interfacing-like stabilizer which is designed to retain its original texture and weight after washing. It won't soften or disintegrate as most of the tear-aways do. This is desirable especially in knits and light-weight fabrics which need stabilization after washing. It is undesirable in sheer fabrics, where it shows through; a wash away would be better, as it would disappear.

Heat away: Available under several different brand names, these will disappear when ironed with a hot iron. The fabric and threads must be able to withstand the heat required to remove the stabilizer, but are very good for fabrics that cannot be soaked or washed in water.

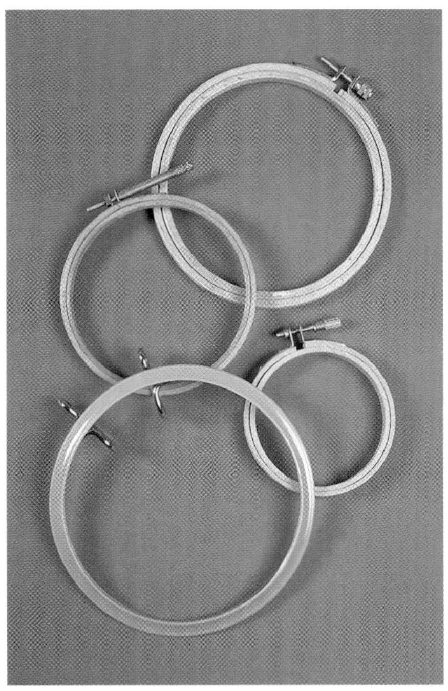

"Sticky Stabilizers": These can be a wash-away stabilizer or a tear away. They have an adhesive applied to them that allows the fabric to hold its position without the top hoop. These work very well on fabrics (such as terrycloth, velvet or satin), where the hoop marks are sometimes difficult to remove. These are put into the hoop, the protective paper removed, and then the fabric placed in position.

Paper stabilizers: Stitch & Ditch or other paper stabilizers are designed to be stitched over to prevent tunneling or puckering of fabric, but they are inexpensive enough that we need not feel guilty about throwing them away after using them.

Hoops: Machine embroidery hoops are necessary to hold the fabric taut when sewing free motion. They can be made of wood, plastic, or plastic and metal. They need to fit under the needle on your sewing machine, otherwise you have to take out the needle every time you place the hoop. They can be any size, from 4" or 5" to 8" or 9". Any bigger will only "bump" into your sewing machine. We most commonly use a 5" or 6" hoop, usually the spring variety. These are the ones with a solid-colored plastic outer hoop, usually purple or red, and a metal spring inner hoop which you "release" into place. The spring hoops are easy to re-hoop, when moving from one area to the next, and are forgiving when lumps or beads get in the way. This type of hoop can usually be moved to the next spot in the sewing machine without removing the work in progress. Wooden hoops are also often preferred, especially when a "tight" hooping is necessary in sheer fabrics. You can wrap the inner hoop to give a better "hold."

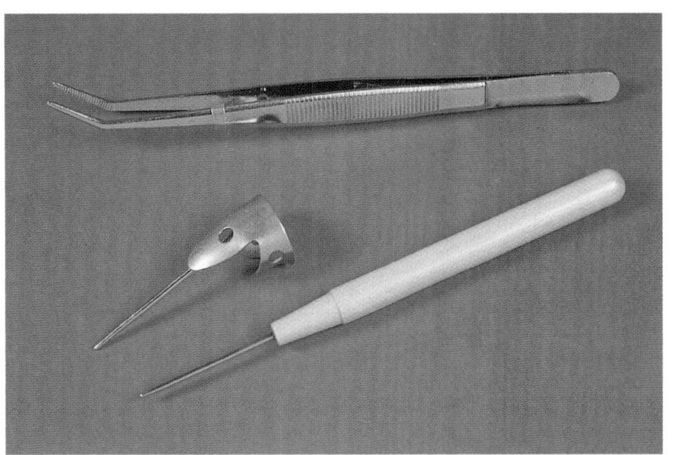

Tweezers/trolley needle/stiletto: Sounds vicious! Actually, these are any number of instruments we use to hold the various threads, ribbons, fabrics or gremlins in place, while we stitch them down.

Serger tweezers: These come with your serger, or can be purchased at any sewing-machine store or most fabric stores. They differ from "eyebrow" tweezers in their length. Serger tweezers are 5" to 6" in length. They're great to hold "things" near the needle, like beads, while we stitch them.

Trolley needle: A blunt needle attached to a curved piece which slides onto your finger. It is great to nudge things under the foot or hold them in place.

Stiletto: A blunt long needle with a handle. You may find them decorative, in brass, with a cap that fits over it when not in use. Useful to hold things or push them under the presser foot.

Snag it tool (or snag nab it): This tool is like a miniature latch hook, or the snag nab it is like a big needle with a cross hatch on one end. Both of these allow the end of the thread, or snag to be pulled through without damaging the base fabric. A small crochet hook can also be used if either of the other two are difficult to find. They are very useful tools to have next to the sewing machine or near your dressing area.

Glues and adhesives: There are many different glues and adhesives available today for our sewing purposes. They can be grouped a couple of ways: spray versus pourables; temporary versus permanent. There are several types of glues available in stick form or in the regular "squirt" bottle. There are also temporary spray adhesives that are useful.

Temporary adhesives: Whether spray or stick form, or pourable, temporary adhesives are intended to hold the fabric in place while we sew it. Be sure that whichever you choose is designed for you to sew through. If it isn't, it will often gum up your needle. The manufacturers of these products are well aware of how a sewer does not like the needle gummed, so they have made a concentrated effort to eliminate this problem.

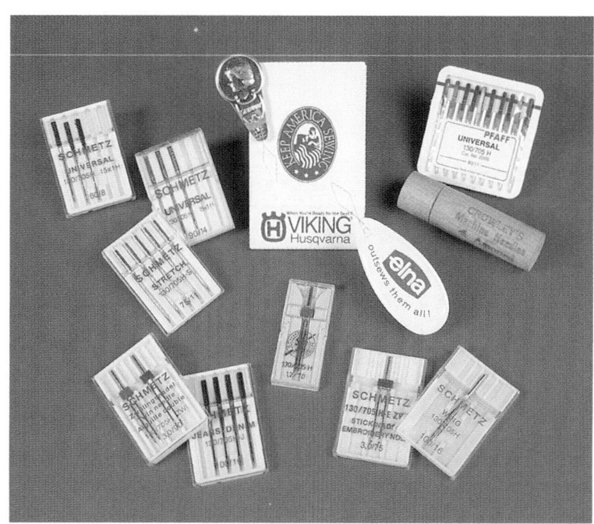

Needles:

In doing decorative work, specialty needles play an important part in making a perfect finished project. Schmetz manufactures the largest variety, best quality needles for our specialty sewing needs. We mention several special types, some of which you may or may not be familiar with. Needles, like all other sewing supplies, are taking great leaps to keep up with sewers' needs.

Double needles: Come in widths from 1.6 to 8.0. When we talk about this width, we are meaning the measurement between the two needles on the single shank that fits into the slot to hold the needle in the machine. The 6.0 and 8.0 double needle are useable in the new machines that have a 6-9 millimeter stitch width available. Some machines have a double needle button on the machine. This is a safeguard so that the machine will not make a wider stitch width than the needle allows. If you use too wide a double needle, or too wide a stitch with the double needle, the needle will break as it "bumps" on the needle plate hole edge. Check the width of the double needle versus the needle hole in the stitch plate if you have doubts. Several of these needles are also available in different sizes. (A 4.0/80 and a 4.0/100 have the same distance between the two needles, but one uses an 80 needle; the other a 100).

Wing needle (or hemstitch): This needle comes in two sizes, 100 and 120. These are relatively large-size shafts with a "wing" on either side. A large needle is used because the purpose here is to leave a "hole" in the fabric after the stitching is completed. These are also available in a double hemstitch (one regular needle and one size 100 wing needle). One of these needles is essential to create machine hemstitching.

Large-eyed needles: We use these when we use a heavier than normal thread (such as jeanstitch, topstitch, or buttonhole). These can be either a topstitch needle or a metallica needle. The topstitch needle is available in size 70 to 110 to accommodate different thickness of thread. The metallica needle is available in size 80 (and soon in size 90). It is designed for use with the metallic threads so popular today.

Spring needle: This is a needle with a small spring attached to it. This is good for free motion work, where the feed dogs are lowered. It allows excellent visibility but prevents flagging of the material being sewn. There are several types of spring needles available—universal, denim, quilting, stretch, and machine embroidery.

Universal needles: Available in size 65 to 120. These are used for general sewing and where we do not specify a specific needle. A good quality needle is an asset for all sewing, and the needle must be changed frequently, as that tiny point can dull or burr easily. There are general rules about changing needles for each project, or with each eight hours of sewing. Just remember it is not a point to brag about having the same needle in your machine for a month or years!

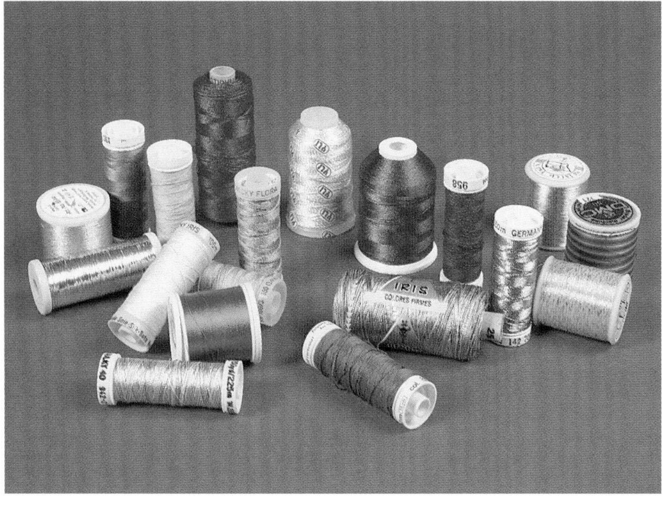

Threads:

In our projects, you will see such threads as cordonnet, buttonhole, topstitching, and jeanstitch mentioned. These are a similar weight of thread, whether they be polyester, cotton, or cotton-covered polyester. They are a heavier than normal thread to be used when the stitching is meant to show or stand out; hence, the names imply. Different companies and time frames used the above terminology.

Invisible or monofilament thread: This is a synthetic thread in two colors, clear or smoke. It is used when we want hidden stitches or when a lot of colors of fabric are being used; it saves changing thread color a lot. It tends to blend in with the background. It can be used in the needle or bobbin case. The new monofilament threads are very fine and flexible.

In our enhancement work, we also talk about different threads such as cotton embroidery, rayon, or some of the yarn types. They will be explained in the specific area of use.

Feet:

Since the original sewing machines didn't do anything except a straight stitch, they came with a variety of different feet and accessories to expand their capabilities. This photo shows some of the "deluxe" accessory options available!

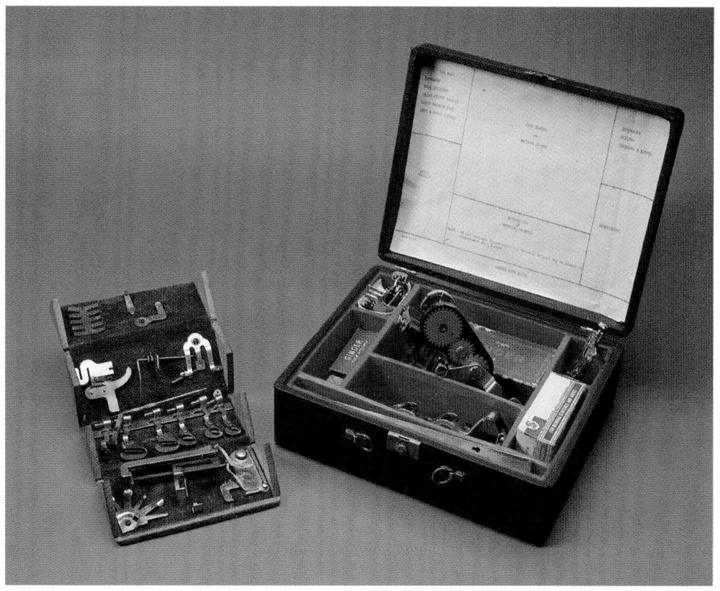

Appliqué or open-toe appliqué: An appliqué foot has a channel on the underside that allows the decorative stitch to move along with the feed dogs, and not jam as it might with the basic foot. The open toe appliqué has the center portion cut out. This allows for greater visibility when sewing with this foot.

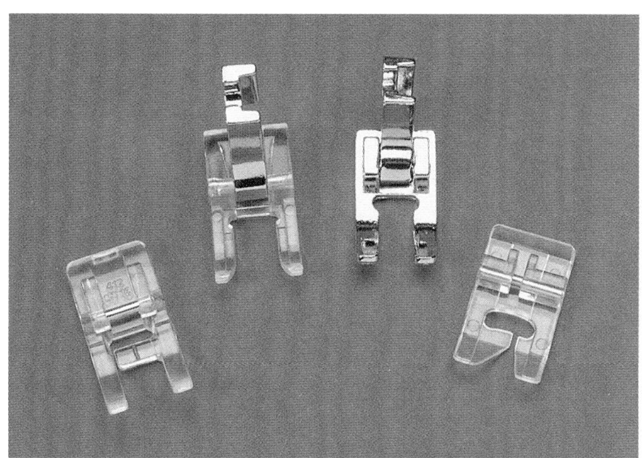

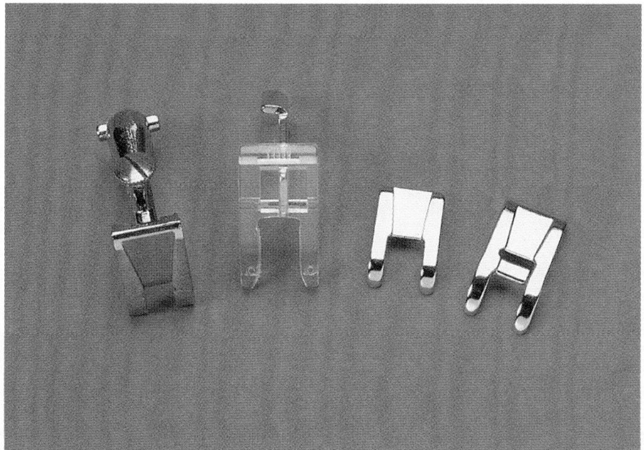

Darning or free-motion foot: The feed dogs are usually down, or covered when this foot is in use. This foot "floats" about 1/4 inch above the area being sewn, and the sewer is guiding the fabric. It sometimes has the front section cut out for greater visibility. The purpose of the foot is to provide freedom of movement of the fabric, but prevent flagging (or bouncing) of the material being sewn.

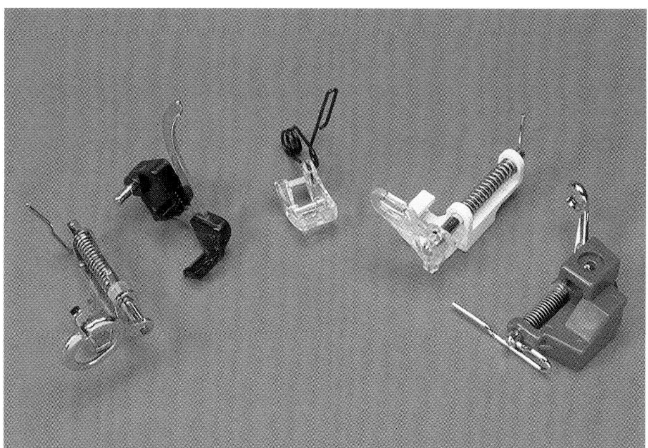

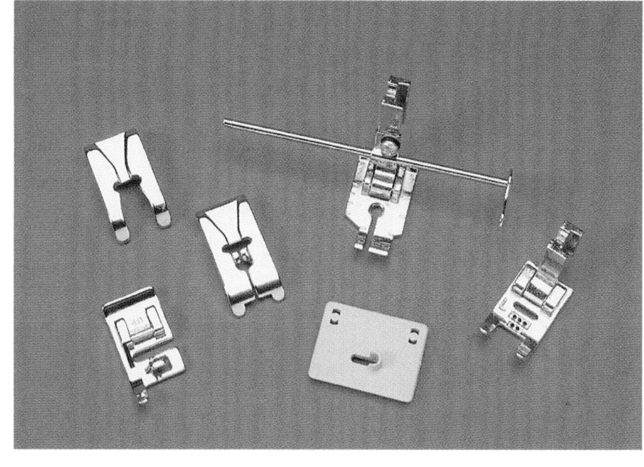

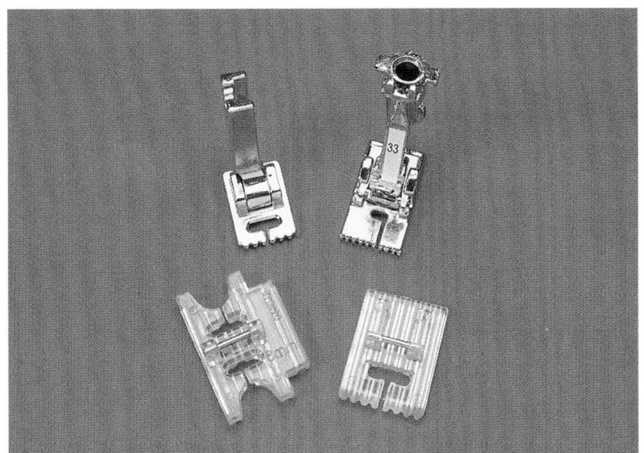

Pintuck: Pintuck feet have channels on the underside which help in positioning pintucks. They come in sizes 3, 5, 7 and 9. The 7 and 9 are designed for fine pintucks in light-weight fabrics, the 5 for medium weight, and the 3 for heavy fabrics. These are used in conjunction with double needles for machine-made pintucks. The center channel allows the fabric to raise as it is sewn with the double needle. Then the side channels serve as guides for spacing future pintucks. Cording can also be placed under the channel being sewn for greater height on the pintucks.

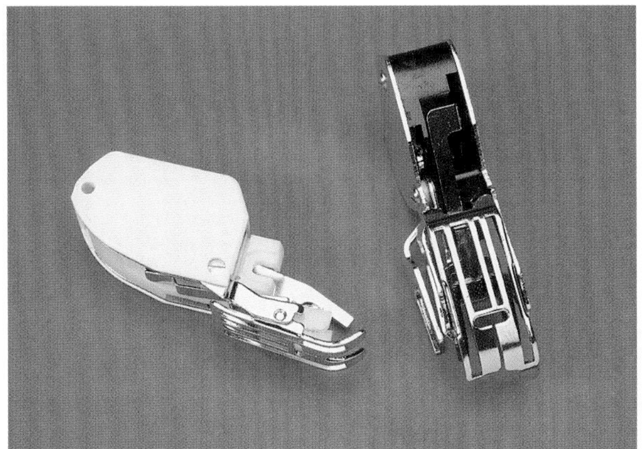

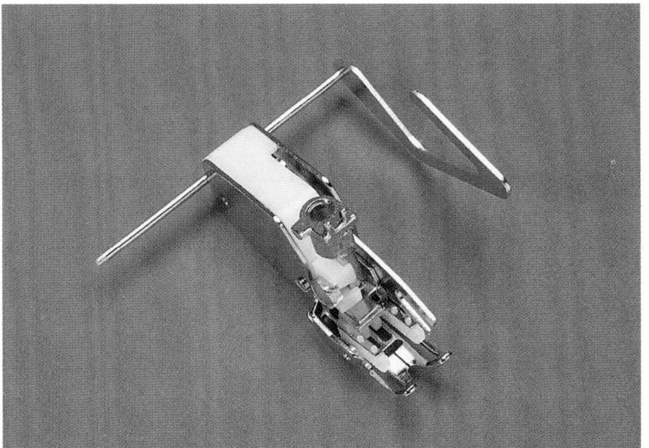

Walking (even feed) foot: This attachment provides a top set of feed dogs to assist in "even feed" of the materials. One sewing machine company has one built into its machine; the other companies provide them as accessories. These are useful when sewing on several layers of fabric (such as quilting through all thickness), sewing on slippery fabrics, matching plaids or wherever there may be increased friction between layers of fabric.

Sewing machines: We have tried to indicate the minimum and optimal sewing machine requirements needed for each project. While a particular stitch may be the best, another more basic stitch like the zig zag can often be substituted.

Lace

The term lace covers a broad range of open work ornamental fabrics and trims created from twisted threads, looped, knotted and intertwined to form patterns. Technically, that differentiates lace from open-textured woven fabrics, such as gauze; from knotted openwork such as net and macramé; and from crochet and knitted openwork, in which the fabric is formed by looping a single thread by means of a hook (crochet) or long needles (knitting).

All of these techniques are capable of producing delicate, lace-like fabrics that are often grouped with true laces. Also closely associated with lace are certain kinds of embroidery such as filet, buratto and tambour work; forms of embroidery on a net base, and drawnwork, where threads are drawn from the fabric; and cutwork, where areas of the fabric are cut out. In all cases, the remaining empty spaces are usually filled in with embroidery.

There are two true types of lace: needlepoint and bobbin or pillow lace. Needlepoint lace was created by one thread using a parchment paper base, where the design was drawn and the single thread was stitched creating the design. Bobbin lace is created with a number of spools called bobbins (as many as 1,200 in elaborate examples). The threads are pinned onto a pad (hence the reference to pillow lace) and knotted and plaited, twisting the threads to create the pattern.

Lace has evolved through the centuries, with a lace-like trim showing up as early as 4000 B.C., through handmade delicacies affordable only by the richest of societies in the 1700s, to machine-made lace available to everyone in the 1800s. In the 1700s, lace was often valued more than jewels because it was all handmade and couldn't be duplicated in any other way, whereas jewels could be copied in paste versions that could pass for the real thing.

By the 1800s, machines were invented to create lace that was a very close imitation of handmade lace. By the mid-19th century, all varieties of laces were made in huge quantities. No longer was it exclusive and only for those with great riches. What had once been out of reach was now readily available.

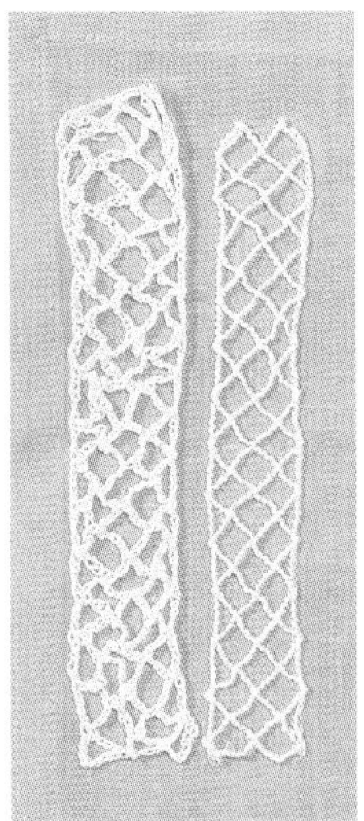

Hand-crochet lace

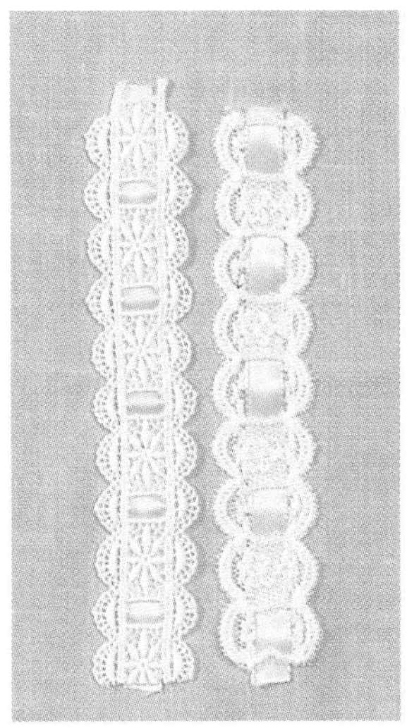
Beading lace

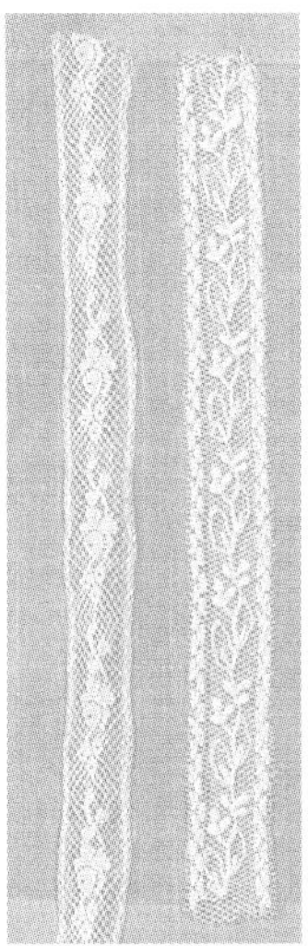
Insertion lace

Edging lace

The variety of laces, named for the centers where they were produced, originated from the different European countries. They were made of the finest threads that could be found and artistically created by professionals. Popularity of the particular laces varied with time, honoring a particular town and country as the most desirable for a time, and highlighting a different type the following year. The most famous originated in Italy, France and then in Flanders. These were widely copied.

Most lace falls into these groups:

French lace is widely used for the techniques we refer to as "French hand sewing by machine" or "heirloom" sewing. These are delicate laces, usually cotton or cotton with a small percentage of nylon for strength.

Val lace, short for Valenciennes, is a narrow flat lace with a fine floral design on netting. It can be a beading lace, a lace with slits through which a ribbon can be laced.

It can also be an insertion lace, usually narrow, with two straight, finished selvage edges used to join two finished edges of fabric, or two laces, or laid on top of the fabric to achieve the same effect.

Or it can be an edging lace, with one selvage edge, straight, to be inserted in the seam or sewn to an edge, and with one decorative edge with scallops or other edge stitches.

The Swiss are famous for embroidered trims, often referred to as lace. These are fabric-based embroidered trims. We will duplicate these delicate, beautiful trims in the embroidery chapter.

Spanish lace is a heavier look, often executed in black. Cluny lace is similar; coarse in texture, it is made with cotton-like threads or yarns. The effect is similar to hand-crocheted lace.

Crocheted lace: During the Renaissance, both peasant women and ladies of the court produced imitations of European lace. One example, Irish lace, was introduced into Ireland about 1820 but also was made throughout Europe. Hand crocheting is beautiful. As with any hand technique, it is time consuming. Crocheted lace is open in texture and can be very delicate, as would be suitable for a christening gown, or more coarse in texture, as compared to some of the finer, imported laces. The delicacy or coarseness of crochet lace is a direct effect of the weight of thread used in its construction.

Battenberg lace is created with a special tape which can be shaped to form curves and is then held together and the open areas are filled in with free motion stitching.

Most laces are available either as edgings, from a scant 1/4" to 3" or 4" wide, or as yardage, 36" or more wide. Yardage sometimes has a finished edge, with a scallop or other such decorative border, or it may have only selvage edges.

In our Lace chapter, we will show you how to duplicate the look of needlepoint and bobbin lace, crocheted edgings and Battenberg lace edgings. We will also show you how to re-embroider lace yardage. In other chapters, we will show you drawn thread work and cutwork embroidery.

Nightshirt embellished with machine sewn, chrochet edging and trim

Our first lace project can be completed on almost any sewing machine. It makes a delightful open work crochet lace, for an edge and for insertion.

Materials needed:

Super Solvy by Sulky (a water-soluble stabilizer)
White 100% cotton machine embroidery thread 40 wt. or rayon machine embroidery thread
Pattern for nightshirt
Linen or linen-like fabric as called for in pattern
Regular sewing thread to match linen fabric
Sewing machine with straight stitch, zig zag and 3-step zig zag

1. Measure your garment or pattern to determine how many inches of lace you will need. On our night shirt pattern, we decided to put insertion lace on either side of the front placket, on the pocket and an edging lace around the collar. The collar lace was specifically shaped for that particular collar. We'll cover that shortly. We began by measuring the length needed to go on either side of the placket and across the pocket.

2. We need to stitch a base for our final zig zag stitching. Because all the Super Solvy will dissolve, we need a base thread for our stitches to hang on to once the backing is gone. The stitch we used is a 3-step zig zag. This stitch is on most machines and has three stitches in the zig and three in the zag. Your instruction book may call it a serpentine stitch. (If you don't have this stitch, substitute a regular zig zag.) Begin by folding your Super Solvy into fours, so you have four layers. You can cut these layers into strips, about 2" wide, depending on how wide you want your strip of lace to be. Overlap

them end to end as needed, as you sew. Set your stitch length at (3), and your stitch width to the widest setting (4 to 9), depending on your particular machine. Thread your machine and bobbin with the cotton or rayon embroidery thread. Stitch one row of the three-step zig zag the length you determined you needed by your measurements.

3. Stitch a second row, having the points overlap just slightly. An open-toed appliqué foot will help you stitch accurately.

4. Continue several rows, until you have reached your desired width. We did four rows.

5. If this is to be an insertion lace, even on both sides, stitch a row of regular straight stitches, slightly overlapping the points of the outer edges of the three-step zig zag rows.

6. Now we're ready to cover these stitches with a narrow zig zag. Set your machine for a regular zig zag, (a single stitch in the zig and the zag), width 1.5 and length 1.5. These settings are approximate. You may need to vary them slightly on your machine. Stitch as shown, from one end to the other.

7. Return, completing the next row.

8. Continue until you have covered all the rows, and then cover the straight stitched outer rows.

9. To stitch our collar lace, you need to begin by tracing your collar pattern onto Super Solvy, using a water-soluble or air-soluble marker. Trace the stitching line, not the cutting line.

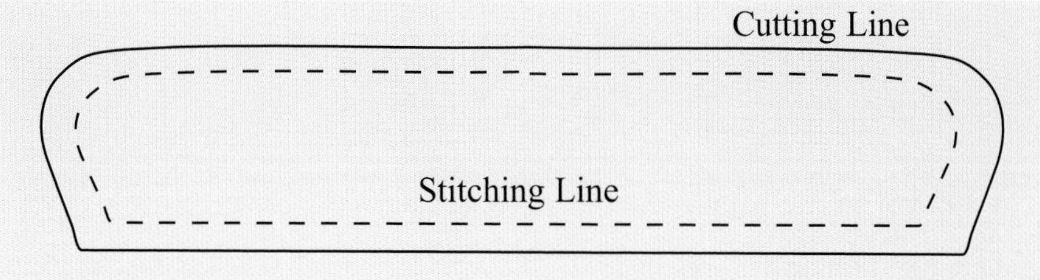

10. Following the previous directions for our insertion lace, stitch the three-step zig zag, and the straight stitch, following the outline of the collar.

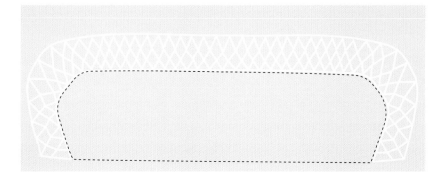

11. Complete by stitching the zig-zag stitch over these stitches, as we did before.

12. Remove the Super Solvy by soaking it in water, according to the package directions. Rinse several more times to remove the stabilizer. Block, by laying out the lace on a towel and shaping it to lay flat. Allow to air dry or, if you're impatient as we tend to be, lay a press cloth over your lace and iron it dry. If it is stiff, there is still stabilizer remaining. It will go away when the garment is washed or dry cleaned.

13. Make your nightshirt according to pattern directions. Before sewing the pocket to your nightshirt, apply the lace. Stitch it in place using a small zig-zag, length 2, width 2. Your placket lace can be placed on top of your fabric as we did, or set it between two finished edges, making an open area.

14. To attach your collar lace, make the collar according to your pattern directions. Stitch the lace to the outer edge, using a small zig zag, length 2, width 2.

Quick Project

Picture Frame Mat

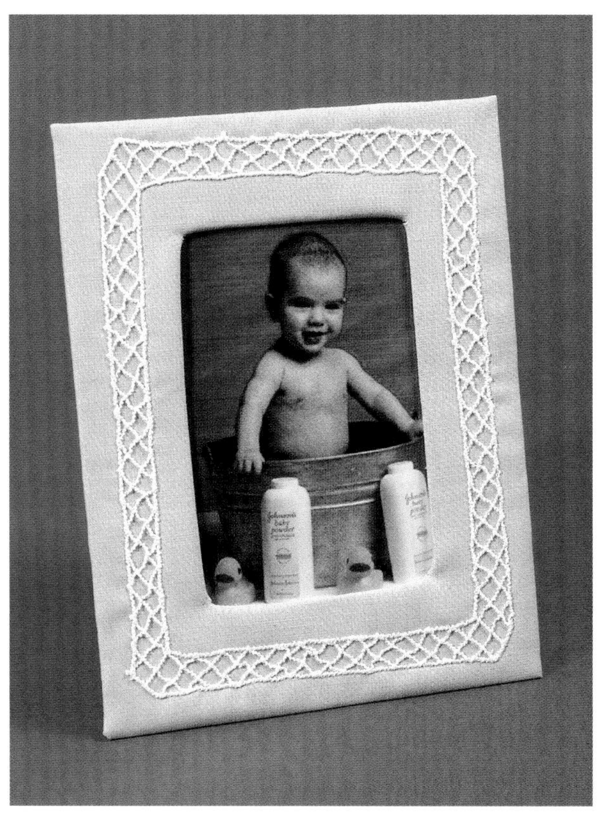

Would you like to practice? Not quite ready to jump in there with a whole garment? Then give crocheting by machine a try on this smaller project. Try a mat for the picture of the favorite person in your life.

Materials needed:

Super Solvy by Sulky (a water-soluble stabilizer)
White 100% cotton machine embroidery thread 40 wt. or rayon machine embroidery thread
Pre-cut picture frame mat or cut your own
(Optional) linen or linen-like fabric the size of the mat, plus 2"
Regular sewing thread to match linen fabric
Sewing machine with straight stitch, zig zag and 3-step zig zag

1. Trace a rectangle 1/2" in from the inner edge of your mat on Super Solvy, as shown. Following the preceding directions, make a rectangle of lace, three rows wide, with a row of straight stitching on each side.

2. Cover your mat with linen if desired, in which case you will lay your finished lace on the fabric and zig zag it in place, as we did on the nightshirt. The alternative would be to glue it in place directly on to the mat board.

Crochet-look Scalloped Edging on Lingerie Bag

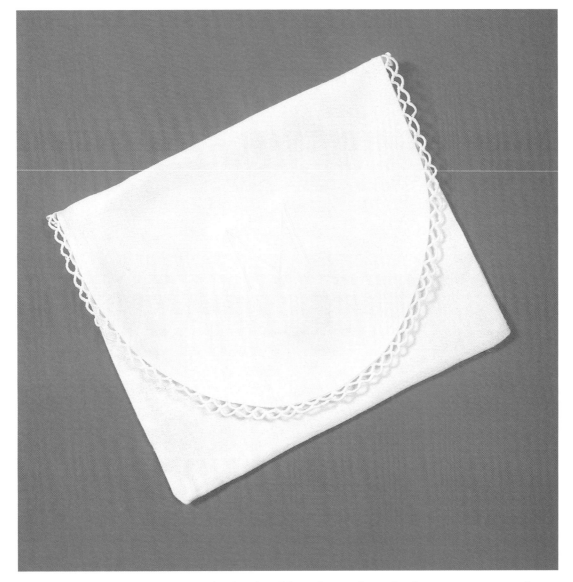

Another great way to get the look of hand crocheted edgings is to stitch a scallop stitch over a "gimp" cord. "Gimp" simply refers to a base cord the other stitches form over. For this technique, you need a sewing machine that has a built-in satin-stitch scallop.

Materials needed: Super Solvy by Sulky (a water-soluble stabilizer)
1/2 yard 54" linen or linen-like fabric
100% cotton machine embroidery thread 30 wt. or rayon machine embroidery thread 40 wt.
Water soluble or air soluble marking pen
Sewing machine with a built-in scallop stitch
Open-toe appliqué foot
White Cordonet topstitching thread or crochet thread to be used as gimp thread
4" x 4" square of tear-away stabilizer

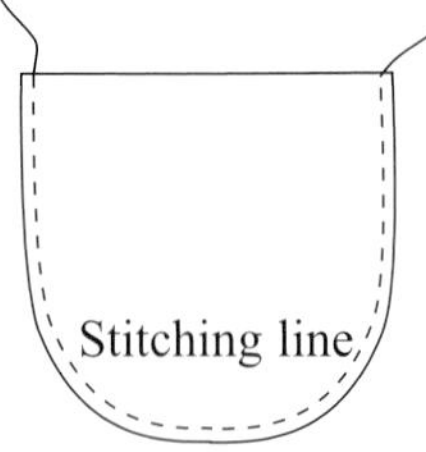

1. Cut your linen into four pieces, 11" x 14". Set two aside. Using the pattern given, cut the other two pieces. Place right sides together and stitch as shown, using a 1/4" seam allowance.

2. Trim with a pinking shears, turn and press carefully. Now we're ready to stitch our crocheted scallops.

HINT: When you trim a curved edge with pinking shears, there is no need to snip into the seam allowance. The pinked points serve this purpose.

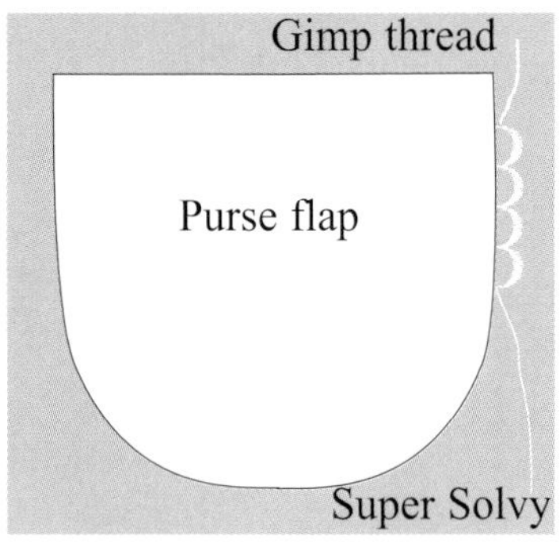

3. Set your machine for the scallop stitch. Follow the directions in your instruction book, but it is usually set at a short length, .05, and widest width, 4-6. You may want to practice a few inches on a scrap before you start on your bag flap. Thread the machine with 30 wt. thread on top and in the bobbin. If we simply stitch our scallops without the gimp thread, they will "fall apart" when we remove our stabilizer. Therefore, we stitch over the Cordonet gimp thread. Place four layers of Super Solvy under the finished edge of the bag flap. Lay the gimp thread under the presser foot and stitch the scallop stitches as shown, just catching into the edge of the fabric, with the bulk of the stitching being off the edge of the fabric, on the Super Solvy. Sew slowly and use something like a large pin or awl to "nudge" the gimp thread into place as you sew. Do not cut off the gimp thread tail.

4. Stitch a second row of scallops, as shown, just catching into the first row. Again, leave the gimp thread tails. This thread is the backbone of our scallop edging. To prevent our stitches from "falling apart," thread these tails into a hand needle and weave them back into the scallop or the hem.

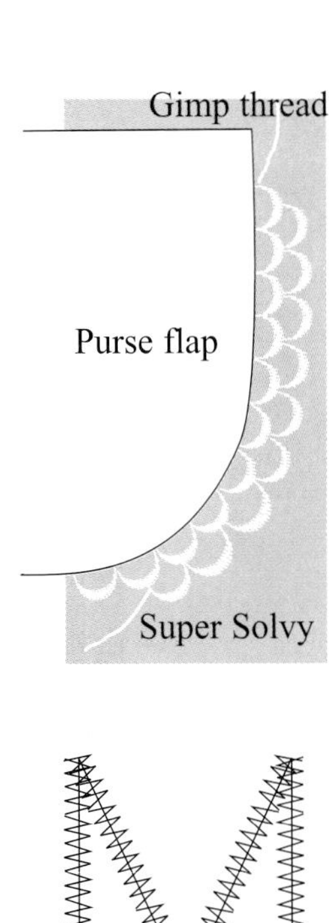

5. We added a simple block satin stitched monogram. Using a water soluble or air soluble marker, draw your letter.

(HINT: If you have a computer, choose a simple type style, set it at the largest size, and type your letter. Print it out on your printer and you have a pattern). Set your machine for a satin stitch, zig zag, set at stitch length .05 and stitch width as wide as it will go, 4 to 6. Place the tear-away stabilizer underneath, and stitch the letter.

6. Reduce the width of your zig-zag stitch to 2, and stitching over a gimp thread, stitch down the center of the previous row of satin stitching.

7. To finish your bag, take the two pieces you set aside. On one, press under a 1/4" hem, then 1/4" again, on the long 14" side and stitch.

8. We'll stitch a French seam to have a nice finish. To do this, place your hemmed piece wrong sides together with your other 11" x 14" piece and stitch with a 1/8" seam allowance, as shown.

9. Next, turn it right sides together and press. Stitch with a 1/2" seam allowance as shown.

10. Place the side with the raw edge wrong sides together with the wrong side of your finished flap, and sew a French seam, as above. Press.

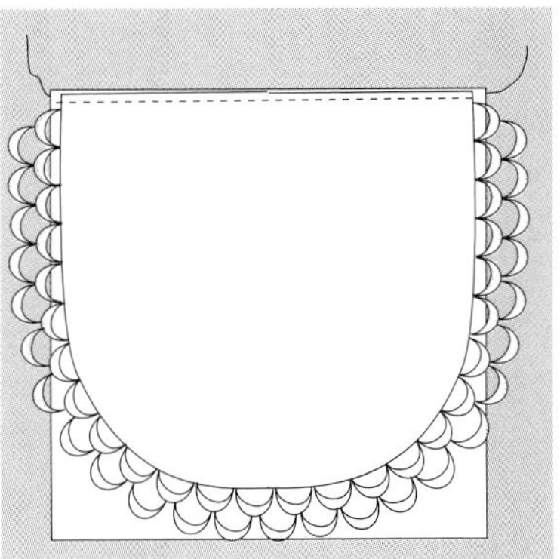

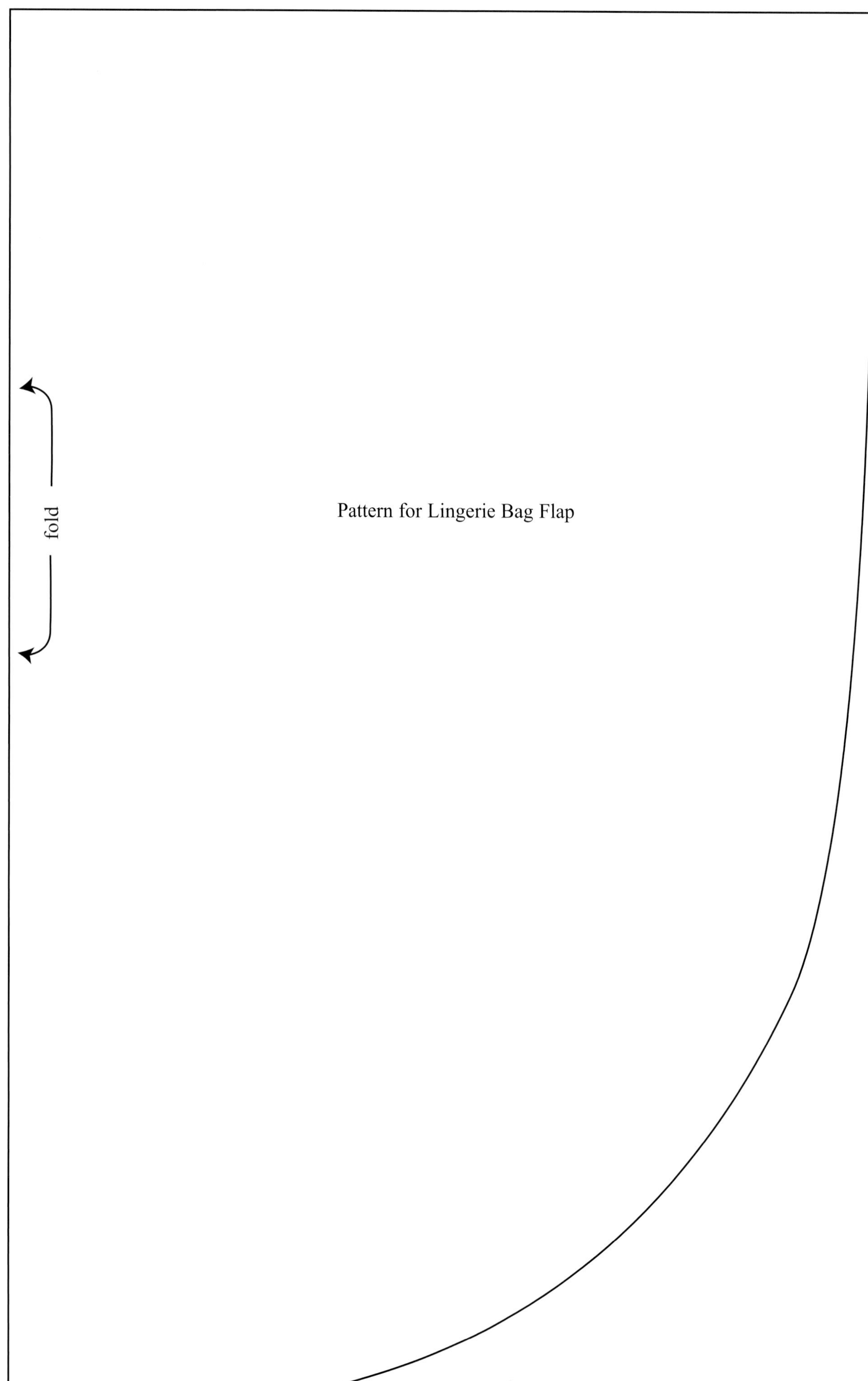
fold
Pattern for Lingerie Bag Flap

Corner Motif on Napkins

Materials needed:

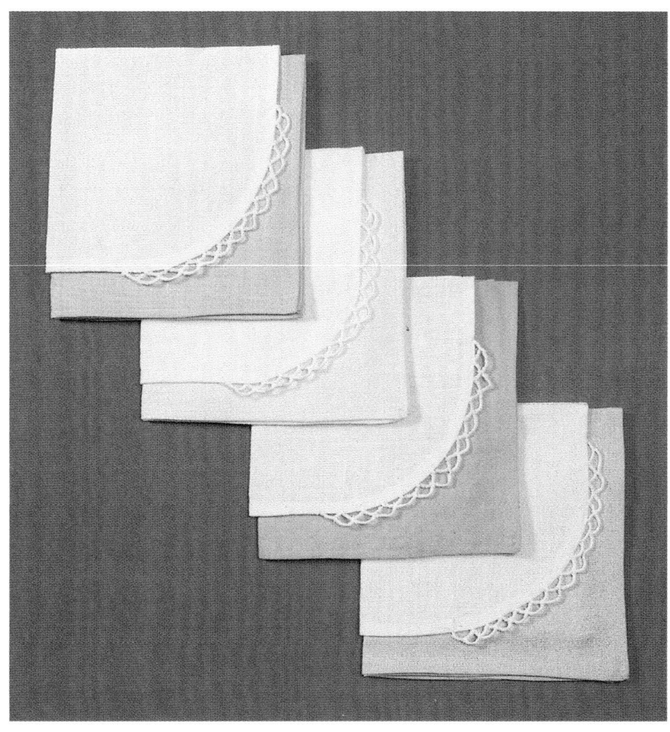

14" to 20" square of linen or linen-like fabric for each napkin (14"-15" for luncheon size, 20" for generous dinner size)
30 weight sewing thread to match
Super Solvy by Sulky (a water-soluble stabilizer)
100% cotton machine embroidery thread 30 wt. or rayon machine embroidery thread 40 wt.
Water soluble or air soluble marking pen
Sewing machine with a built-in scallop stitch
Open-toe appliqué foot
Cordonet topstitching thread or crochet thread to be used as gimp thread

1. Begin by rounding one corner of your napkins. Cut a paper pattern first; try a mixing bowl, an embroidery hoop or whatever you have handy that is 6"-10" across and round. Once you're pleased with your curve, cut one corner of all your napkins at once. Following the directions on page 62, make mitered corners on your other three corners. Stitch your hem in place, using a straight stitch. Lay your curved corner on four layers of Super Solvy and, following the directions for the lingerie bag, stitch a corner motif as shown. Do not cut the gimp threads. Because they are the backbone of our scallops, they need to be left long and threaded onto a hand needle, and threaded back through a scallop or the hem of the napkin.

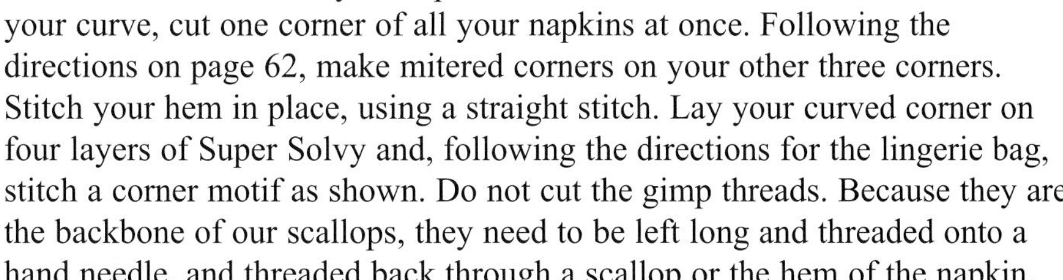

2. Remove the Super Solvy by soaking it and rinsing it in water, and block to shape.

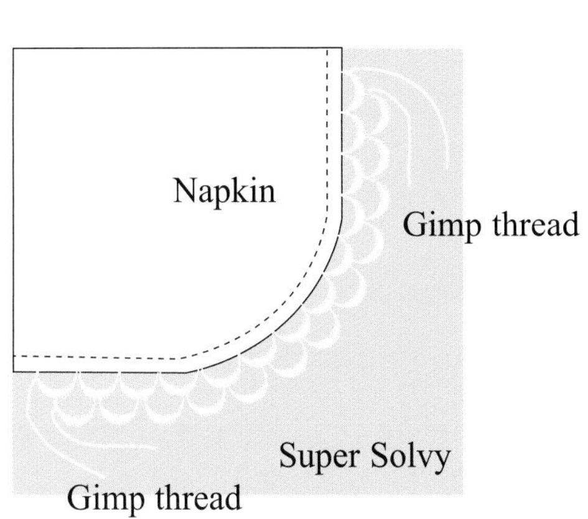

Hint: A wonderful way to use these napkins is with a colored "liner" napkin. Simply make a plain napkin, in multi-colors as we did, or all one color, about 2" bigger. Place them under your decorated napkin and fold them together. The fun part of this is that the colors can be citrus, like ours for summer luncheons, red, green or blue for the holidays, or "pumpkin" colored for fall get-togethers.

Making Heirloom Lace

We are referring to this type of lace as heirloom lace, as it is the type you might use for a christening dress, first communion dress, an old fashioned lacy blouse, or a night gown. It is what was originally the needlepoint or bobbin lace. We will be building it on a base of fine netting with decorative stitches from our sewing machine. Any stitches can be used, even so-called functional ones. The more elaborate the stitches, the better. There are two parts to this section: the lace, which you can apply to anything, and the doll's dress, which will be continued in other chapters. We've also divided the materials-needed list into two sections: Those which you need for making the lace, and those you will need to make the dress.

Materials needed for making lace:

1/2 yard English netting or illusion veiling (found in the bridal department)
30 wt. cotton machine embroidery thread or rayon machine embroidery thread
Super Solvy by Sulky
Sewing machine with at least a few stitches other than straight and zig zag

Materials needed for making doll dress and bonnet:

Doll dress pattern
100% cotton batiste as called for in the pattern
2.0 twin needle
(2) spools 60 wt cotton thread
Pintuck foot for your sewing machine
Wing needle size 100 or 120

1. We used our laces to make a dress for our old-fashioned china-headed doll. We began by measuring the pattern to determine how much of what kinds of lace we would need. The bottom of our skirt was 45" around. We wanted our edging lace to be gathered, and about 1-1/2" wide. Because we were going to gather the lace, we made 90" (double the skirt width). At the same time, we did the length to edge her bonnet. We needed several short pieces, about 6", of edging lace for the edges of the sleeves. We needed two long pieces of insertion lace, the length of her skirt for the center of her skirt detail, and matching pieces for her sleeves. While you may not want to make them all at once, we found it easier to plan them out and complete them all at one time. We cut our netting into strips about 3" wide, and pinned each one to four layers of Super Solvy. To join the netting and Super Solvy where we needed longer strips, just overlap them slightly. At the same time, set up a short strip as your practice piece. We had so much fun trying out the different stitches, we had trouble getting started on the actual lace!

2. Begin by stitching a row of stitching down the center of what will be the insertion lace for the front of the gown.

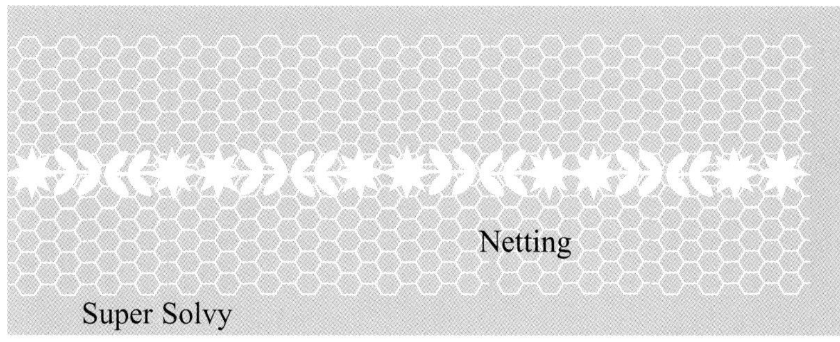

3. Choose a different stitch and add a row on each side. Use the same stitch on both sides to give a balanced (equal) look to your insertion lace.

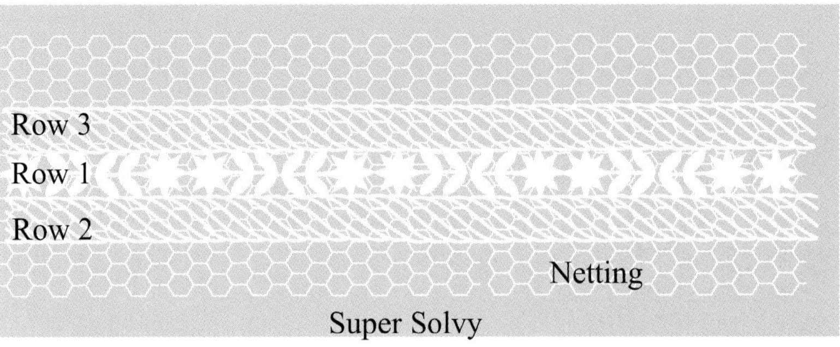

4. Depending on the width you want your lace and the width of your sewing machine stitches, continue adding rows until your desired width is reached.

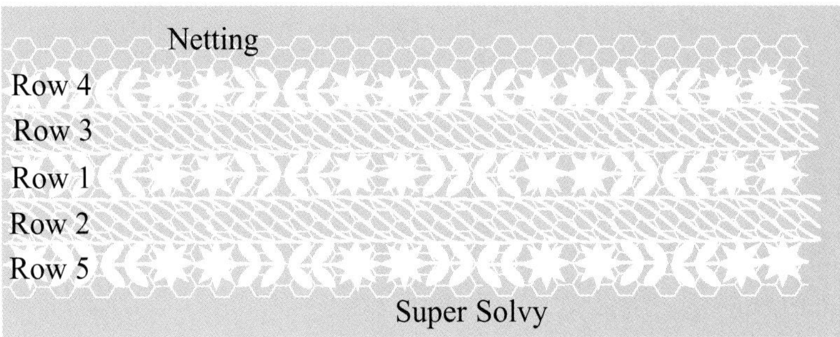

5. Make your edging lace the same way, but add a scallop stitch for the outer edge.

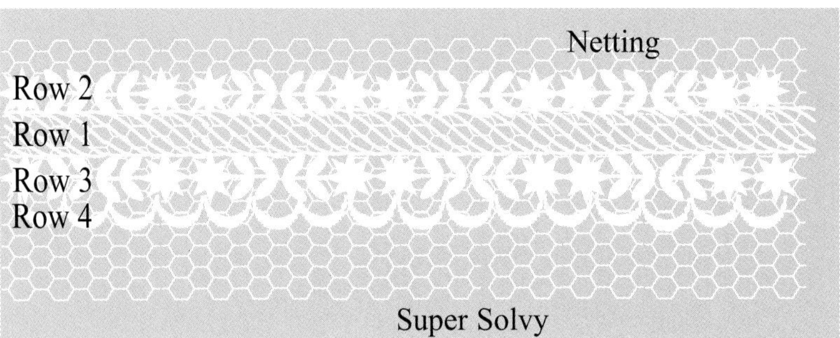

6. Soak all your lace in water, rinsing well until all the Super Solvy is gone. Lay the lace on a towel to dry. Trim the netting off around the scalloped edges on the edging laces. The remainder of the laces can be trimmed now, or sewn in place on the garment, and then trimmed. The strongest is to stitch the untrimmed lace in place with a small zig zag, length 1.5 and width 1.5. Then trim the excess netting. This can be the finished edge, or you can add a hemstitched edging as we did. The directions are on pages 62-63.

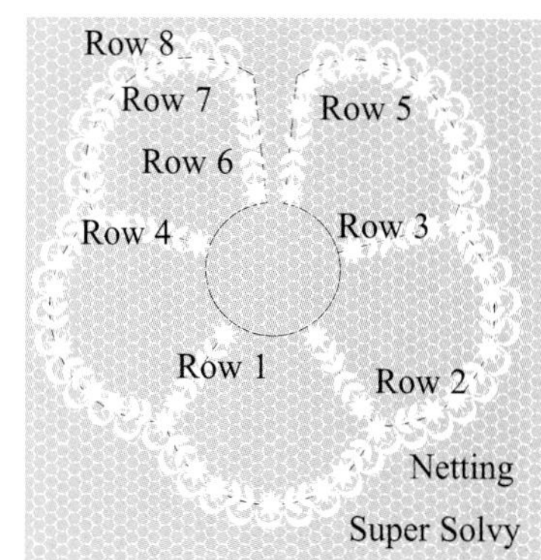

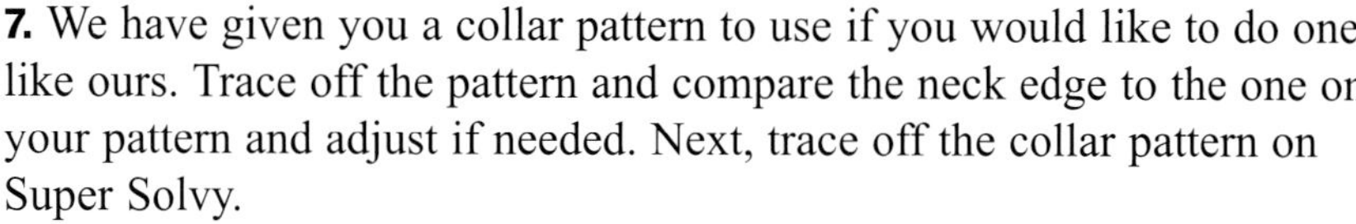

7. We have given you a collar pattern to use if you would like to do one like ours. Trace off the pattern and compare the neck edge to the one on your pattern and adjust if needed. Next, trace off the collar pattern on Super Solvy.

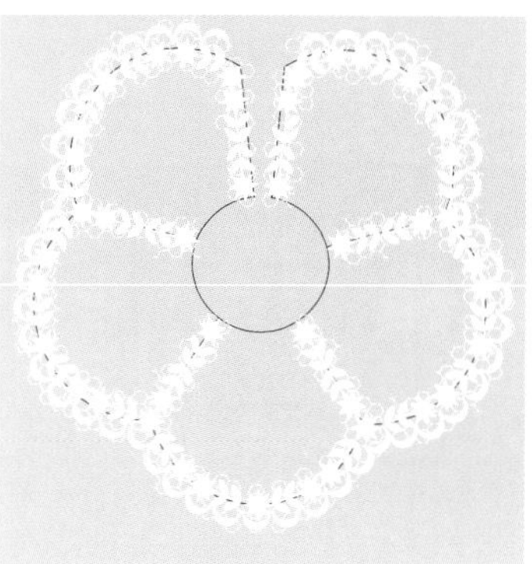

8. Lay a piece of netting on top of it. Stitch the decorative stitches in the order shown.

9. Now you're ready to remove the Super Solvy by soaking it in water and rinsing it well. Shape the lace to the pattern as it dries. Next trim the excess netting from around the lace shape as shown. You have created a custom-made lace creation!

10. Trace the collar shape onto a square of fabric, using a water soluble or air soluble marker. Place your lace on the fabric, using the drawn lines for placement. Stitch the lace in place, using a small zig-zag stitch. Stitch width 2, stitch length 2. Then trim away the excess fabric.

11. We used a hemstitch, with a wing needle, to create Entredeaux while attaching our lace at the same time. See pages 59-60 for instructions. Stitch over the edge, going just on and off the edge of the lace.
Additional instructions for the twin needle stitching are on pages 47-49. We used it to create the fabric for her bodice, and the pintucks embellishing either side of her central skirt motif.

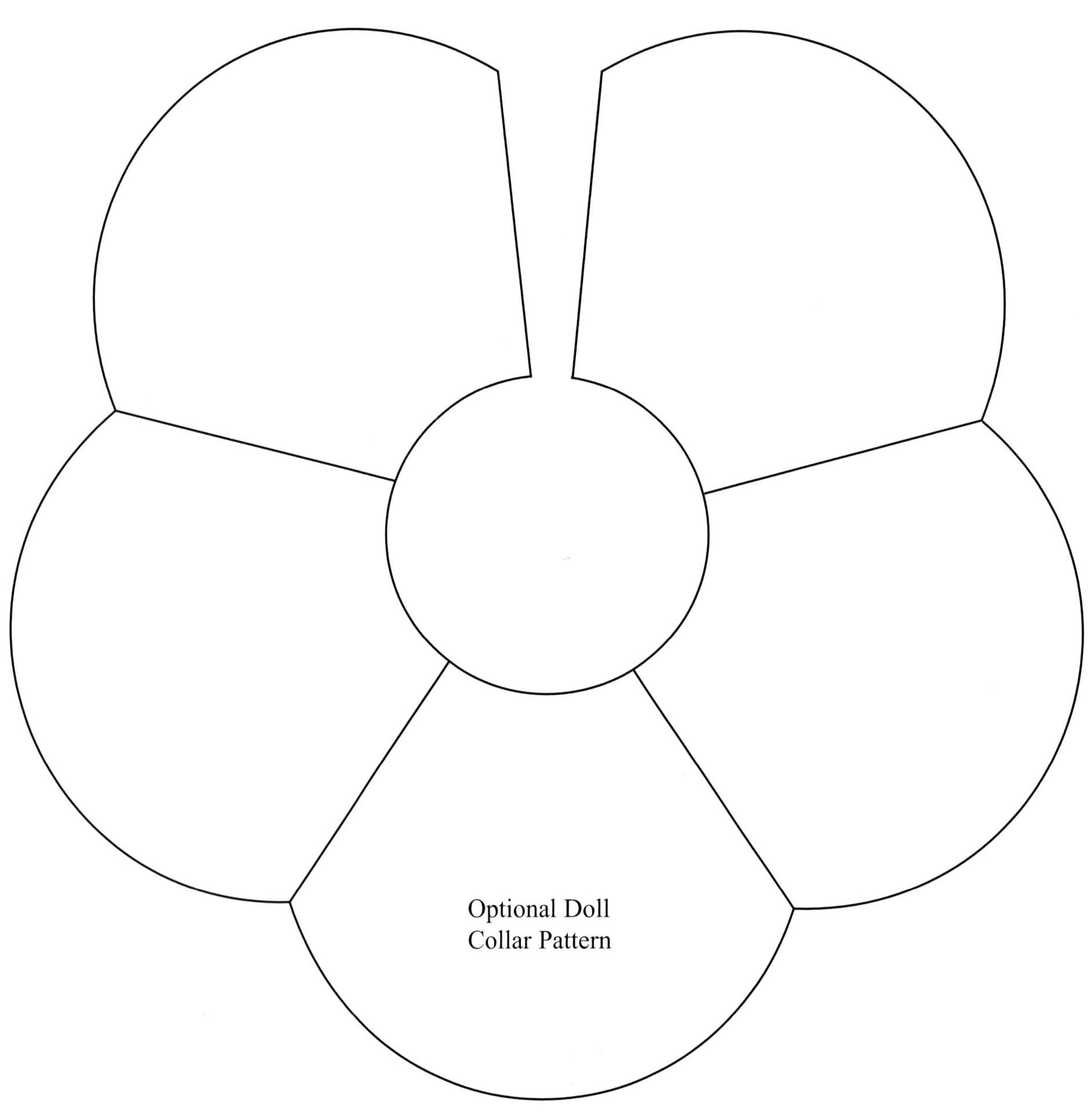
Optional Doll
Collar Pattern

Quick Project

Wedding Hankie/Baby Hat

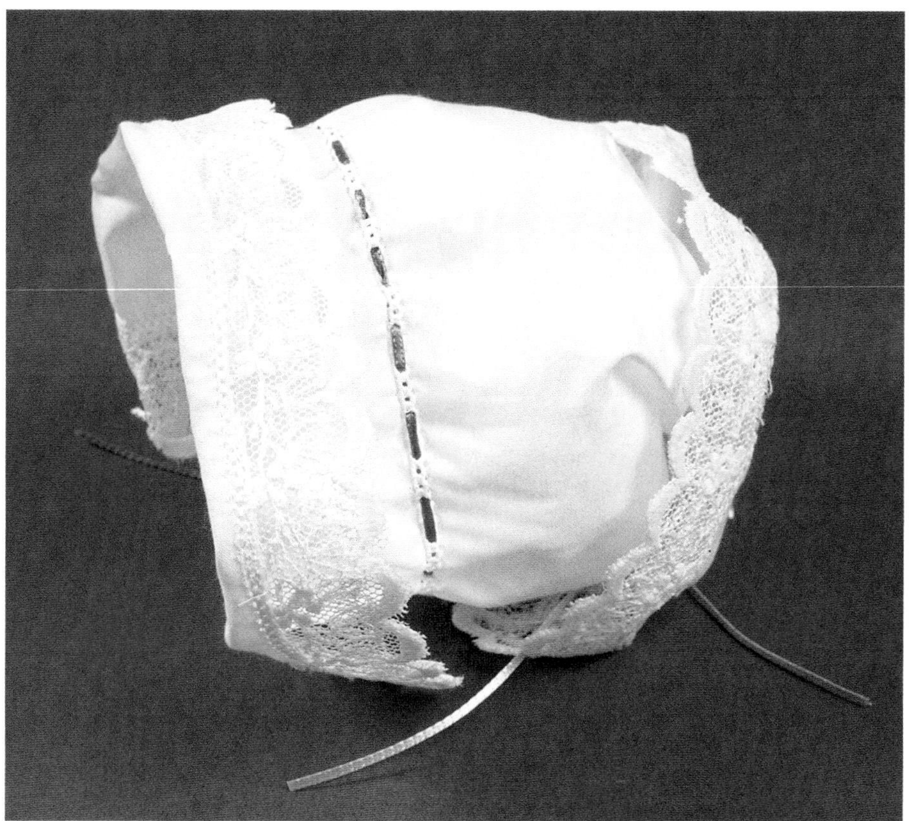

We've seen this idea around for years, with many variations. The basic premise is a hankie for a bride to carry, which can then be converted to a baby bonnet. The reverse is to give it to a baby, to be tucked away later for the grown-up baby to carry at her wedding as "something old" or for the grown-up baby boy to give to his bride to carry. Copy the following poem and tuck it in with the hankie.

A little bit of Lace...

A square of fabric with very special lace,
Threaded with ribbon through the base!
Leave it flat for the bride to carry,
When the day arrives that she does marry.

Then smooth it out and tuck it away,
To await the time on another day,
When a babe is born, to bless her life!
Fulfilling her dream of mother and wife.

Draw up one ribbon, pulling it tight.
Tie a bow, and tuck the ends out of sight.
Fold back the other, where the ribbon lies,
And try it on baby to check the size!

Think, as you tie the bow, on this little face,
Through generations to come, this bit of lace,
will continue the cycle, from baby to bride,
Created with love, persistence and pride!

Materials needed for making lace:

1 strip English netting or illusion veiling (found in the bridal department), 2" x 42"
30 wt. cotton machine embroidery thread or rayon machine embroidery thread
Super Solvy by Sulky
Sewing machine with at least a few stitches other than straight and zig zag
10" x 10" square of batiste or handkerchief linen
60 wt. cotton machine embroidery thread
Wing needle size 100 or 120
1-1/2 yard of 1/16" ribbon, white, pink, or blueSuper Solvy by Sulky (a water-soluble stabilizer)
1/2 yard 54" linen or linen-like fabric
100% cotton machine embroidery thread 30 wt. or rayon machine embroidery thread 40 wt.
Water soluble or air soluble marking pen
Sewing machine with a built-in scallop stitch
Open-toe appliqué foot
White Cordonet topstitching thread or crochet thread to be used as gimp thread
4" x 4" square of tear-away stabilizer

1. Choose a pretty lace design from your samples and make a 42" strip. Stitch it around the 10" square of batiste or handkerchief linen using a small zig zag, width 1.5 and length 1.5. We used hemstitched Entredeaux shown on page 60 next to and slightly overlapping the lace, and we then stitched additional rows as shown, 2 inches in from each fabric edge.

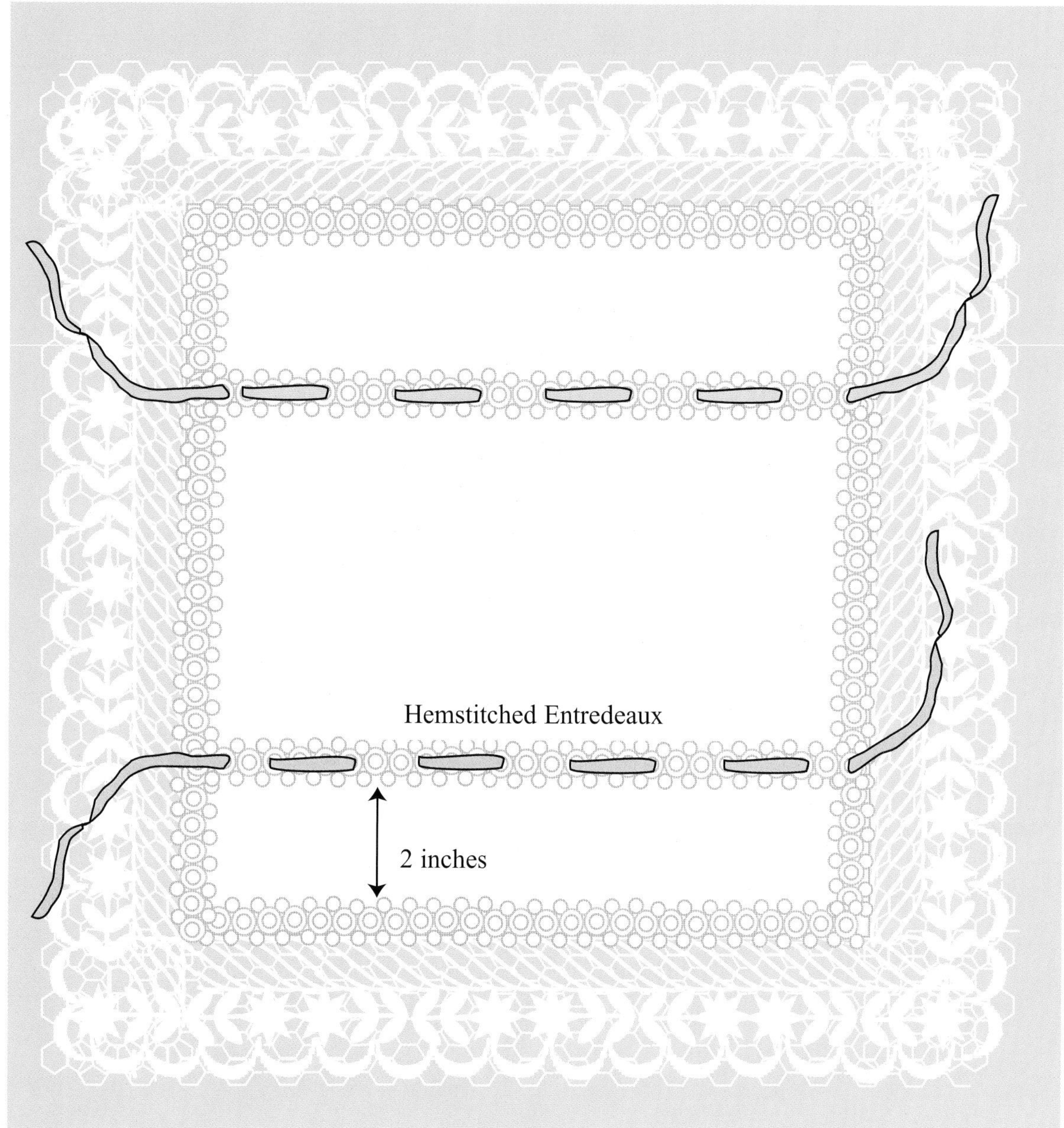

2. Cut the ribbon in half. Thread the ribbon through the two rows of Entredeaux, going into one hole and skipping two. If you do not have the Entredeaux stitch, you could zig zag over the ribbon, creating a casing.

Re-embroidered Lace
Collar and Sash

Re-embroidered lace is simply lace that has been embellished with additional cords, threads, beads, or sequins. It is often used in bridal wear and very expensive. Yardage can run well into the hundreds of dollars. Trims are a little less, but expensive none the less. We chose a less traditional approach for our garment, a young girl's holiday dress. Even the "tom boys," who wouldn't be caught dead going to school in a dress, enjoy dressing up for the right occasions. Christmas, First Communions, bat mitzvahs, and weddings are a few of the occasions in a young girl's life that require a dressy dress. Combine the elegance of a luxurious fabric, we chose velvet, and a custom embellished lace collar and sash, adorned with pearls, and you will win her heart and many compliments! We chose an inexpensive lace; the decision-making factor was a large enough design to embellish, and a stable enough lace to withstand our hooping and stitching. A very delicate lingerie-type lace with tiny flowers would not be appropriate. In that our lace was only $2.99 a yard, we splurged and bought a whole yard so we would have plenty to play with. We limited ourselves to pearls because we didn't want it too "glitzy," but our Quick Project, the "Padded Barrette," shows what a few glitzy beads and sequins added to the basic cord and pearls can do! We had lots of leftover lace and a bit of velvet and our beautiful dress looked so lonesome sitting on an ugly plastic hanger, so we made a padded lace-covered hanger. Directions will follow.

Materials needed:
- Dress pattern with a fairly large collar, suitable for embellishing
- Velvet or other suitable fabric as called for in pattern
- 1/2 yard lace yardage, similar to photograph, with a sufficiently large design
- DMC rayon embroidery floss to match lace
- Rayon embroidery sewing machine thread to match floss
- Pearls for embellishing (hole must be big enough for a sewing machine needle)
- Machine embroidery hoop
- 5" to 6" serger tweezers

1. If the collar pattern is designed to be placed on the fold, make a full-size pattern on paper first. Trace both the sewing lines and the cutting lines. We are making a single-layer collar. Your pattern instructions will tell you to cut two collars and one interfacing. Ignore these instructions and trace the one on lace only.

2. Look at your lace. Is it a one-way design? We don't want upside down or sideways roses! It probably won't be perfectly symmetrical, so you want to lay your pattern piece under the lace and move it around until you find a pleasing spot. We didn't want to cut our flowers in half so we fudged, going in and out around them.

Dotted lines indicate pattern sewing line. Solid lines indicate actual line we followed, according to our lace, for embellishment.

3. Trace the pattern piece for the collar onto your lace with an air soluble or water soluble marker. Be sure to preserve the actual pattern cutting and sewing lines around the neckline, where it attaches to the dress, even when it cuts things in half. We need enough fabric to "hoop." Allow 2" to 3" extra to extend beyond the marked lines.

4. Set up your machine for free motion machine embroidery, see pages 89-91. This allows us to move every which way, to follow the design in the lace. If you've never done free motion sewing, this is an ideal project for you because your mistakes will *not* show! Thread your machine on top, and in the bobbin with the rayon machine embroidery thread. Place your lace fabric in the hoop.

5. Start by lowering your presser foot and taking a few stitches into the lace fabric. Cut off your thread tails.

6. Now we are ready to couch our embroidery floss in place. Lay the end on the lace fabric and take a few stitches to anchor it in place. The way you move the hooped fabric creates a sort of zig zag.

7. Continue, following the outline of your lace, as shown.

8. Stitch your pearls in place as you go, see page 39 for instructions.

9. After we were done, we added an extra embroidery floss line, outlining the outer edge.

10. Now trim away the excess netting and attach the collar to your dress following the pattern instructions.

11. We made a sash by measuring the waist of the dress, adding 3" for overlap and seam allowance, and using that measurement for the length; following the rose pattern in our lace, it ended up about 3" wide. Embellish the lace as above, and then cut it out, leaving 1/2" seam allowance all the way around. Lay it on a piece of velvet the same size, and baste in place, or use spray adhesive such as KK2000 by Sulky. Place it right sides together with a strip of lining the same size as the sash pieces, and stitch all the way around, leaving a hole to turn on one side. Turn, press and sew hooks and eyes to close, or if you prefer, you could use Velcro. On ours, we followed the rose design in and out instead of stitching a straight line.

Hint: Use a zipper foot on your sewing machine to enable you to sew close to the pearls without getting stuck!

12. For our padded hanger, you will need 2 yards of 1/2" wide ribbon, your lace and velvet scraps, and some scraps of light-weight batting or fleece. Measure the hanger from the center out to the end, and cut two strips of batting that width by about 8" or 10". Roll them up, and baste them so they stay rolled up. Hold a piece of fabric around them and take that distance plus 1" for seam allowances. Cut two velvet pieces that measurement, by the original hanger measurement, from the center to the edge plus 1" for seam allowances. Cut two lace pieces the same size. Baste them together or use spray glue. Fold them right sides together forming a tube, and sew the side and one end. Turn and slip onto the batting roll, and then onto the hanger. Repeat with the other side, and hand sew them together in the center. Wrap your hanger end with ribbon, and use the remainder to wrap around the center of the hanger where you joined the ends, and tie a bow.

Quick Project

Barrette Covered with Re-embroidered Embellished Lace

Use up your scraps or try out the project by making a barrette. We purchased a "form," but you could also use template plastic.

1. Trace off the barrette shape with air soluble marker onto a lace scrap, big enough to fit in your hoop. Following the directions on the previous pages, embellish with cord, beads and even sequins.

2. Finish cutting out the embellished lace 1" bigger all around. Cut a matching velvet piece. Place over the form and hand sew in place. Cut a backing of felt or Ultrasuede, and attach a barrette by hand or with a glue gun.

Battenburg Lace

Battenburg or tape lace has enhanced garments for many centuries. The most common areas to embellish with Battenburg lace have been collars and cuffs on clothing. Doilies and linens embellished with Battenburg lace are also very popular.

The tape used in the construction of Battenburg lace is a delicate cotton. Most common sizes are 1/4" and 1/2". This tape comes in white or ecru, but could easily be dyed to match any other color needed. It is lightly woven and has an almost hemstitch effect down the center. There is Battenburg tape that has two flat sides, and another type that has a picot edging on one side. The latter is handy to use if the tape is on an edge and not being inserted into a seam or piece of fabric. The tape we used had a string on each side to aid in gathering. This helps to create smooth curves. If you are making sharp corners, or 90 degree turns it works best to fold the tape on top of itself and stitch it down.

Battenburg Lace Pillowcase

Materials needed:

2 yards of 45" fabric, cotton or cotton blend
Battenburg tape- approximately 1 yard 1/2" wide straight; approximately 1-1/2 yards 1/2" wide filet edge
Sewing thread to match base fabric
Water-soluble stabilizer
Temporary spray adhesive such as KK2000 by Sulky or straight pins
Hoop large enough to hold most of pattern
Machine embroidery thread (we used a silk finish mercerized cotton) to match Battenburg tape

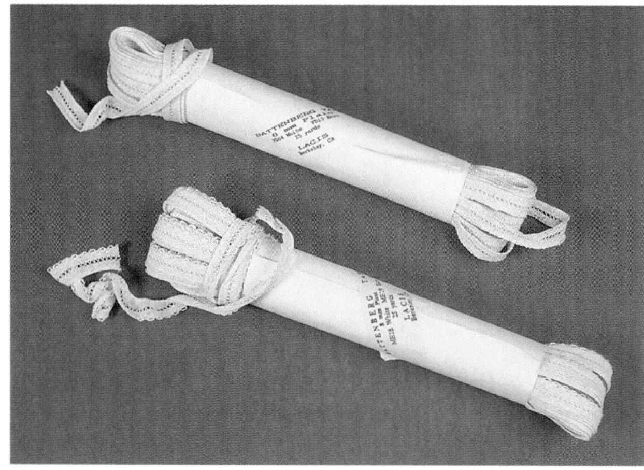

Standard-size pillowcases finished size are 20" wide by 30" long. Cut fabric 41" wide and 32" long. If you are making queen or king-size pillow cases, determine size from pillowcases you already have, or on a purchased package.

1. For a French seam in the pillowcase, sew the one side seam in a scant quarter inch, wrong sides together, then press and turn. Sew a generous 1/4" right sides of fabric together, covering the previous row of stitching. Repeat this same technique for the closed end of the case. Hem open edge by pressing 1/4" under, then another 1/4" under sewing, a double hem.

2. Draw or trace the shape for the medallion in the center of the edging onto a piece of paper.

3. Place the water-soluble stabilizer in a hoop on top of pattern. Either use a temporary spray adhesive, sprayed onto the water soluble stabilizer or pin the straight edged tape around the shape. Pull the gathering thread to help the curves lie flat. If using the temporary spray adhesive, the tape will adhere. If pinning, use enough pins to hold shape. For sharp corners, make a fold in the tape and when stitching, tack the layers together.

4. Fill in the open areas with free motion stitching. Sew right over the water soluble stabilizer, remembering to stitch onto the tape at frequent intervals, and cross over the stitching to help anchor. We did several patterns in a free form design.

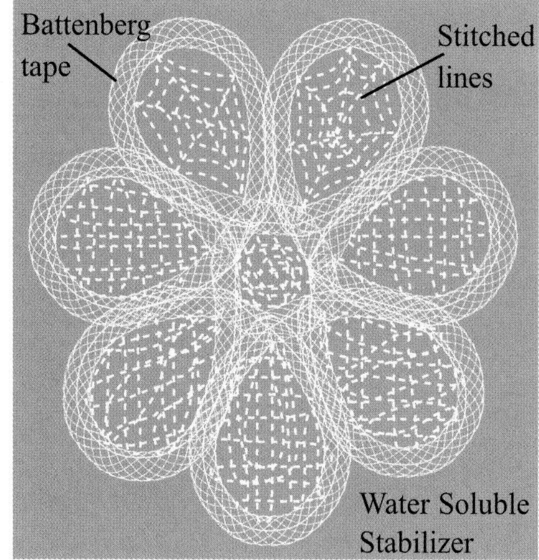

5. Remove lace medallion from hoop and trim away excess stabilizer. Center medallion onto finished pillow case. Stitch around both sides of tape, where it attaches to the fabric, to provide a base to anchor medallion. Cut away fabric under medallion.

6. With the picot edge Battenburg tape, we tucked the raw end of the tape under the medallion, and made l-1/2" scallops along front of pillowcase. We folded the tape at the top of the scallop, and used the gathering thread to help shape the scallops.

7. At the side, we let the tape go straight on the underside of the pillow case.

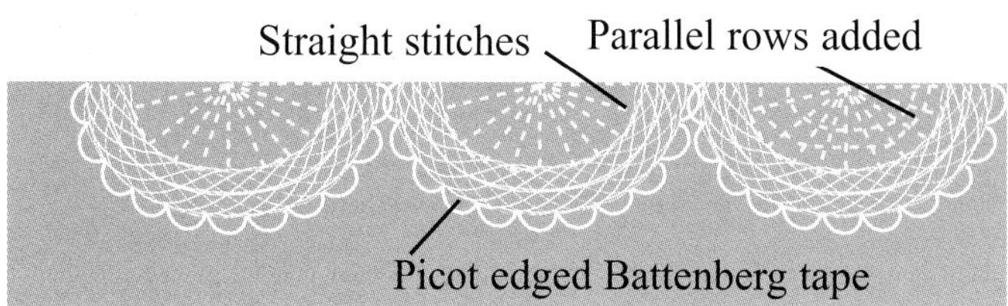

8. The front scallops were filled in with a free-motion "sunray" effect. Start at the center and anchor a couple stitches onto the pillowcase fabric. Stitch straight out, sew over on the tape about 1/8" to 1/3", stitch back to starting point. Repeat until it is filled as much as you like.

9. On the first scallop on either side of the medallion we also did a row parallel to the scallop. This could be done in each scallop if you desire.

10. On the underside of the pillowcase, we attached the Battenburg tape, keeping it straight and using a zig-zag stitch.

11. When you get to the side of the pillowcase, construct the scallops on the other side front as we did in step 5 above.

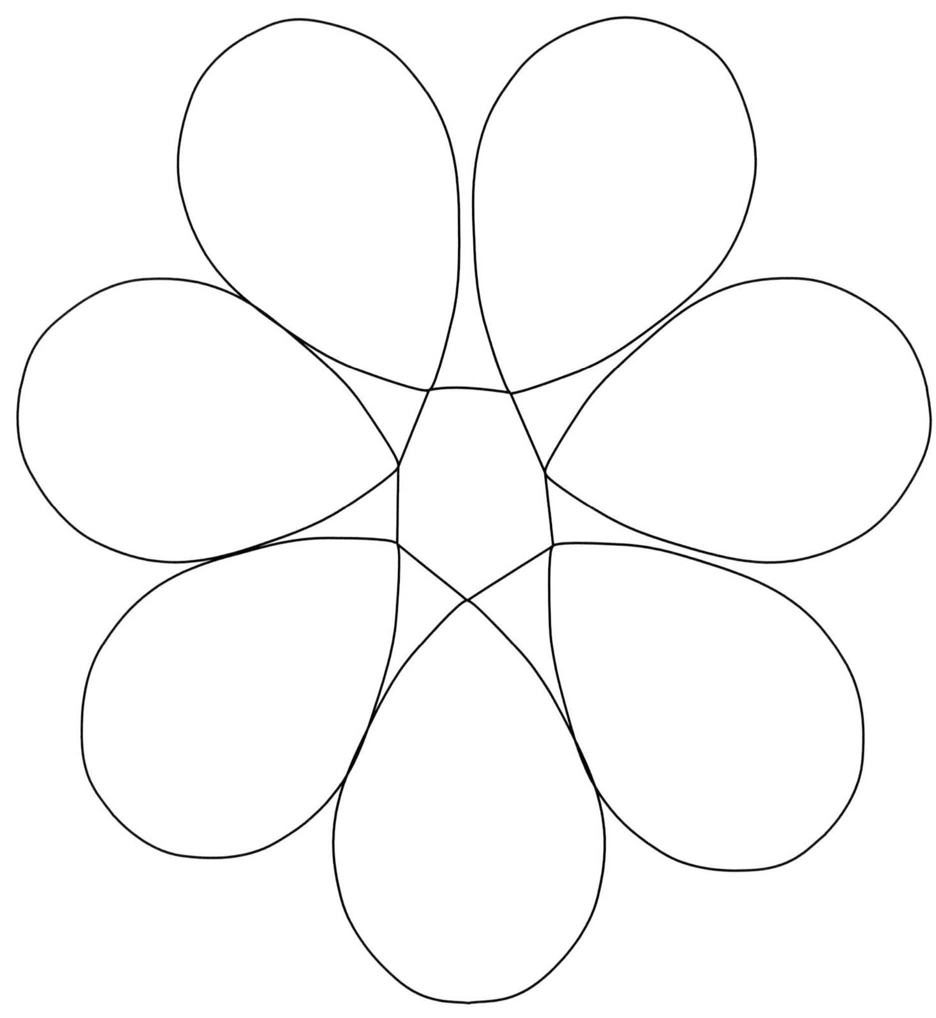

Quick Project

to sew onto T-shirt

Materials needed:

Water soluble stabilizer
Battenberg tape (we used 1/2")
Pattern
Sulky K2000 temporary spray adhesive
30 wt. or 40 wt. machine embroidery thread to match Battenberg tape
T-shirt to sew pocket onto

1. Trace pattern onto paper or make a copy on a copier. We used a basketball shape for this quick project. Could it have had anything to do with watching basketball playoffs at the time?

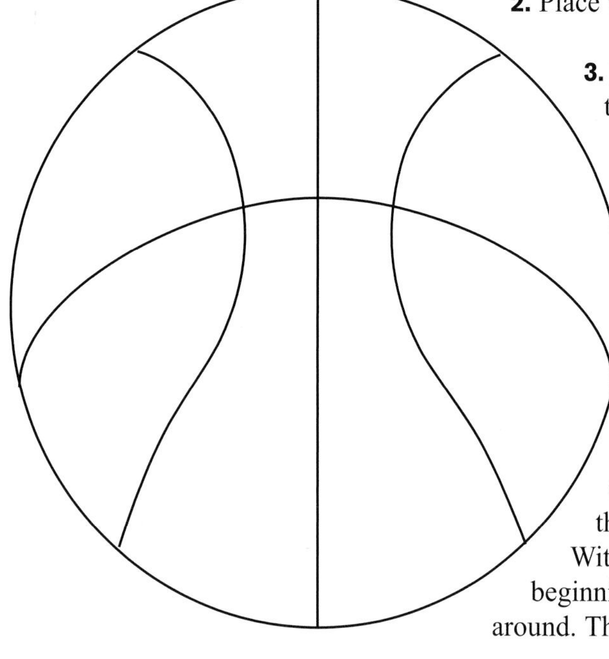

2. Place water-soluble stabilizer in hoop.

3. Lightly spray temporary spray adhesive onto the top of the water soluble stabilizer.

4. Place hoop over pattern and lay Battenburg tape over the pattern lines. Pull on the draw thread to help shape curves. Use a continuous piece of tape as long as possible. Where short pieces are needed, cut them long enough to be tacked onto the adjoining piece. The adhesive will hold the tapes in place, and even allow adjustments if needed.

5. Lift hoop, with tape from pattern. Now let's go to the sewing machine and start connecting the tapes. With regular weight sewing thread to match tape, sew beginnings and ending together on the tape, all the way around. This can be done free motion. Be sure to secure the thread ends when you start and stop. See pages 93-95 for free motion sewing instructions.

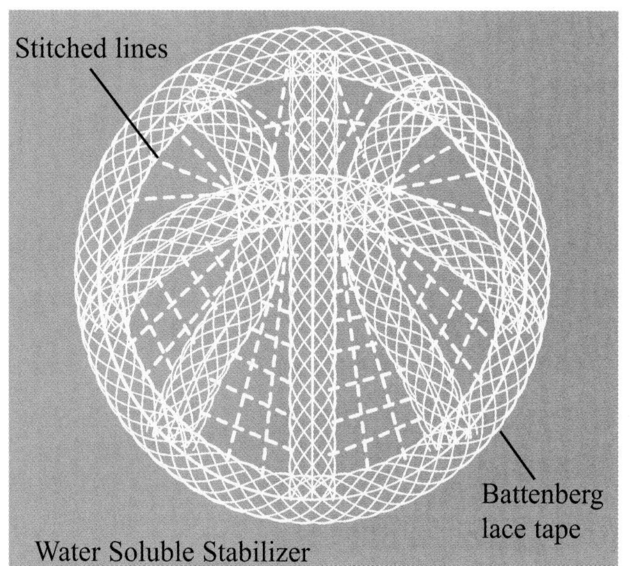

6. Thread machine with machine embroidery thread in both needle and bobbin. If you are working a lot of straight lines, and have an open toe foot for your machine, you can sew the straight lines with feed dogs up. Be certain to tack the threads at beginning and end so they do not fray. If you are making your next row of filling stitches not too far from the last, you can stitch a couple stitches on the tape to get from one stitch area to another.

7. Follow our pattern for the basketball pocket or create your own. We used straight stitching for this project.

8. Wash out the water-soluble stabilizer according to manufacturer's instructions.

9. Sew pocket onto T-shirt and enjoy!

Tucks

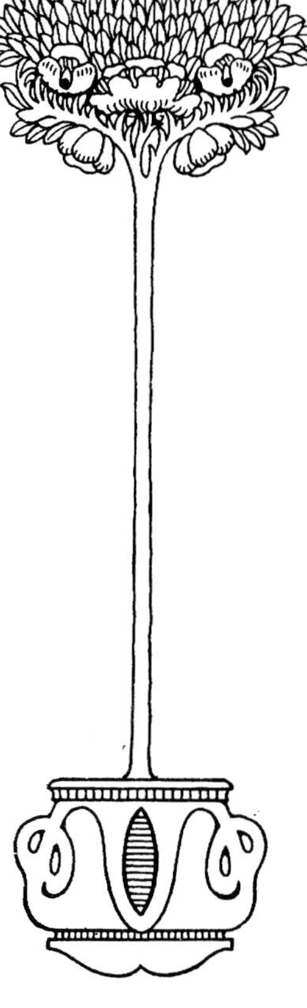

Tucks were probably one of the first fabric manipulation techniques. Formed by folding the fabric wrong sides together and stitching close to the edge, there are many variations and types of tucks that can be formed. The fastest and easiest is also one of the most impressive, pintucks, sewn with a twin needle. We used these on our baby doll's christening dress. We also have an easy way to add basic tucks to any shirt or blouse, shown on our little boy's "Sunday-go-to-meeting" shirt, and more elegant, textured fabric manipulation in our "flip flop" tucks.

Twin Needle Pintucks

The tiny hand-stitched pintucks seen on christening dresses, children's wear, lingerie, and fine ladies apparel were meticulously measured, stitched and pressed for a wonderful textured tone-on-tone look. The modern-day sewing machine and the invention of the twin needle have made them a breeze, accomplished in minutes, rather than hours upon hours. Most sewing machines will accept a twin needle and after choosing the one appropriate for the fabric you are using, you're all ready to go!

Twin needle pintucks on doll bodice

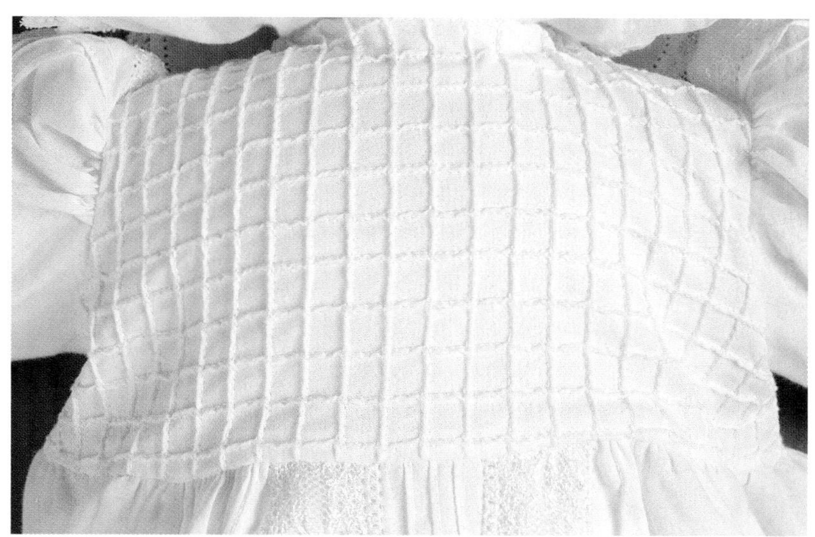

Materials needed: Sewing Machine: Any sewing machine with a front loading or top loading bobbin will accept a twin needle. As you look at your sewing machine, if the bobbin is under the needle (top loading) or in front, below the needle (front loading), you're OK. If, as you look at the machine, the bobbin is on the left hand side, you cannot use a twin needle.

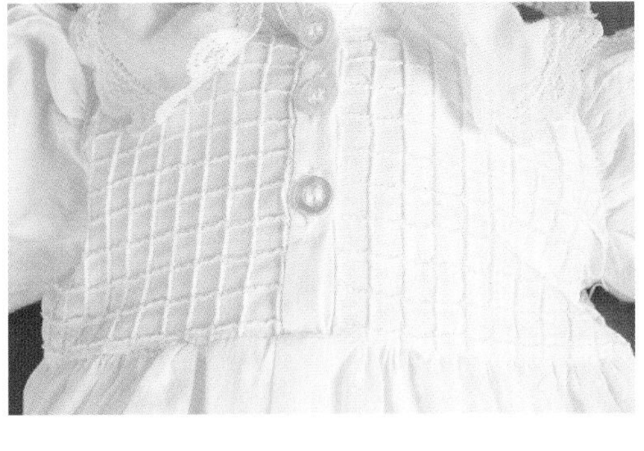

Twin needle size 2.0

2 spools 60 wt Cotton thread

Pintuck foot, see pages 48-49 for details

Preparation: Because the pintucks "take up fabric," we will stitch a piece of fabric, then cut out the bodice pieces. This is the approach you always want to take with a pintucked piece.

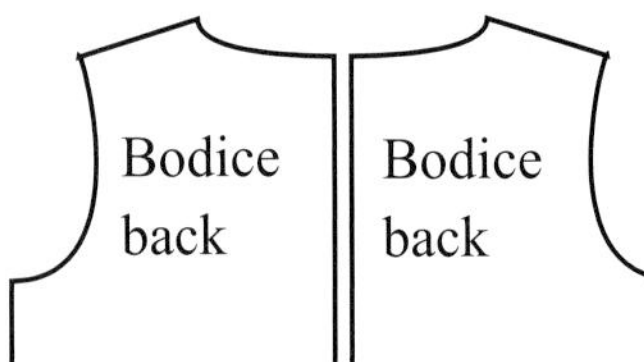

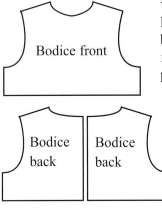

1. Start by cutting a piece of fabric half again the width and half again the length of the bodice pieces. This may be easier if you trace off a second bodice back, and a full-size bodice front, if it is shown on a fold. Be sure the fabric is on the straight grain. We will pull a thread as our guide to start our pintucks.

Bodice back | Bodice back

2. Pull a thread 1" from each edge as shown, as the starting point for the pintucks.

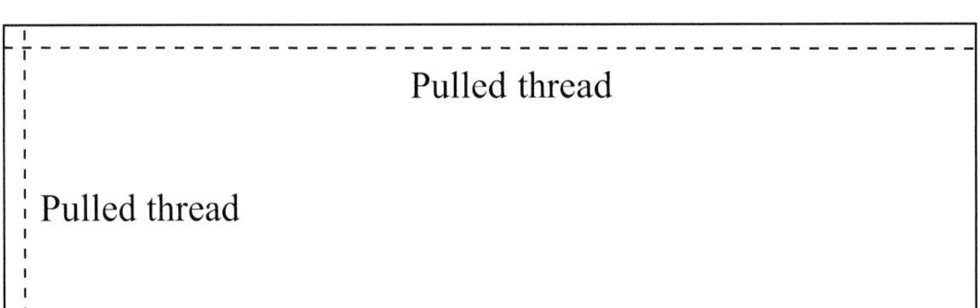

3. Now we're ready to start sewing! Thread your sewing machine with two spools of white thread. The finer the thread the better; 60 weight cotton is ideal. The bobbin should be the same.

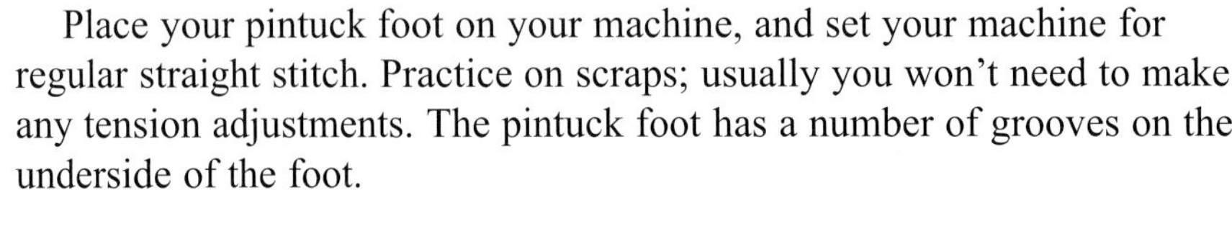

Place your pintuck foot on your machine, and set your machine for regular straight stitch. Practice on scraps; usually you won't need to make any tension adjustments. The pintuck foot has a number of grooves on the underside of the foot.

They are there to space the tucks. The tuck being sewn is in the center of the foot. The second tuck can be sewn in a number of ways. Experiment by placing the first tuck sewn in the groove just next to the center. Then try the next one out; then try the next one, etc. and finally try the edge of the presser foot. We spaced our tucks by placing the previous tuck next to the foot.

4. Beginning on one of the lines created by the pulled threads, stitch the first pintuck. Make a "U" turn, and stitch back doing the second tuck, at the edge of the foot or running it under the foot in one of the grooves. Continue going back and forth, covering the fabric. Check occasionally to see if you have tucked sufficient fabric to lay your pattern pieces on.

5. Now, go back to the other pulled thread and stitch the tucks in the opposite direction. Because you are sewing over the previous tuck, it is important that you stitch all these rows sewing from the same direction. So, at the end of the row, take the fabric out of the machine and go back to the starting end.

6. Lay your pattern pieces on the tucked fabric and cut them out.

7. The pintucks on either side of the skirt lace strips were stitched in the same way, but only in one direction.

8. The hem on the basket lining was stitched using a different stitch. We used a straight stitch scallop, but you can also try some of the others shown.

Straight stitch scallop

Three step zig zag

Serpentine stitch

9. IMPORTANT! - You must narrow the width of your stitch. The exact numbers will depend on your individual machine. Try about 1/2 of your widest width, i.e., if your widest width is 9, try 4.5. If your widest width is 4, try 2. Turn the handwheel by hand toward you and manually stitch through one repeat of the stitch. Be sure the twin needle clears on both sides of the needle plate. If it's touching, make the stitch width narrower. Try your stitch length at 1-1/2. Use your appliqué or satin stitch foot. See pages 13-14 for information on presser feet. Stitch a sample on a scrap two layers thick. Adjust the stitch length until you are pleased with the effect.

10. Prepare the fabric for the hem by folding up a 2" hem and pressing it in place. Stitch your scallop stitch 1-3/4" in from the folded edge. Be sure to stitch from the right side!

HINT: Need to mark a line to follow temporarily? For our hem, measure 1-3/4" from the needle and place a rubber band around your free arm at that point.

Directions for our Christening dress will continue in the hemstitch chapter on page 61.

Quick Project

Doll's Hat

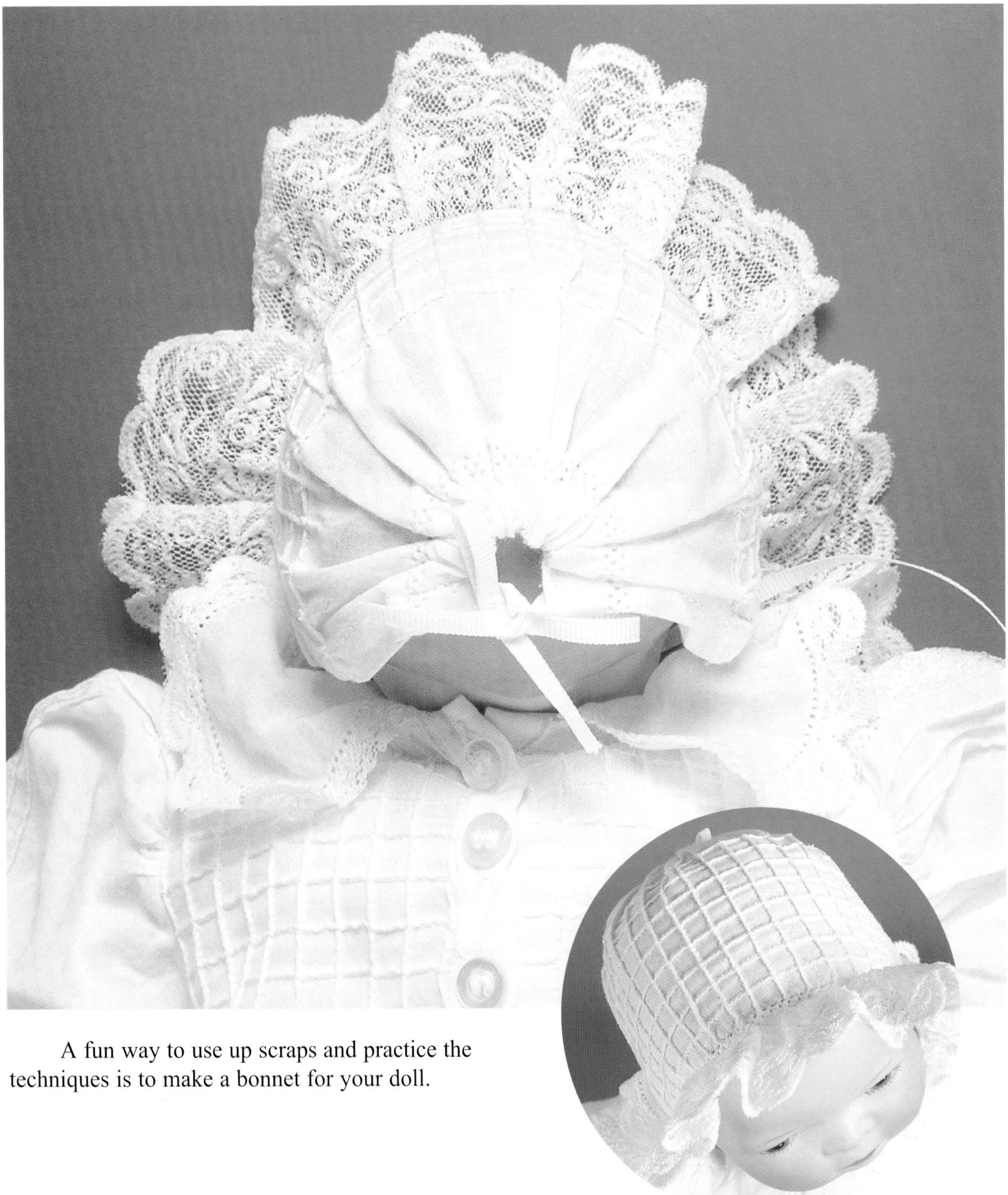

A fun way to use up scraps and practice the techniques is to make a bonnet for your doll.

Materials needed:

1 yard of 1/4" wide ribbon
18" of 2" wide lace
9" x 18" piece of batiste
Sewing Machine: Any sewing machine with a front-loading or top-loading bobbin will accept a twin needle. As you look at your sewing machine, if the bobbin is under the needle (top loading) or in front, below the needle (front loading), you're OK. If, as you look at the machine, the bobbin is on the left-hand side, you cannot use a twin needle.
Twin needle size 2.0
2 spools 60 wt cotton thread
Pintuck foot; see pages 48-49 for details

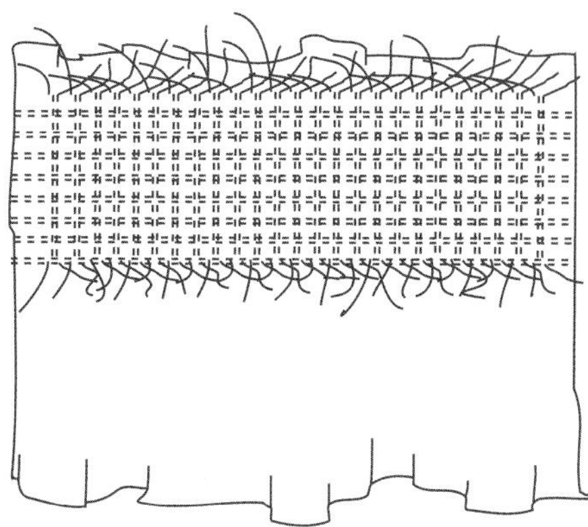

1. Following the directions on pages 48-49, stitch 8 rows of pintucks along the 18" length.

2. Stitch 25 tucks in the opposite direction as shown.

3. Hold it around the doll's head and adjust if needed with more tucks. Hem the short sides.

4. Gather the lace to fit and attach it to the pintucked edge. We used a hemstitch with a wing needle, see pages 62-63.

5. Turn a 1/2" hem up on the un-pintucked edge. This will form a casing for the ribbon on the back of the hat. We stitched this hem with a hemstitch and a wing needle, see pages 62-63.

6. Insert 12" of ribbon into the casing and pull tight. Tie in a knot, then a bow.

7. Cut the remaining ribbon in half and attach it to the front edge for ties.

Traditional Pintucks

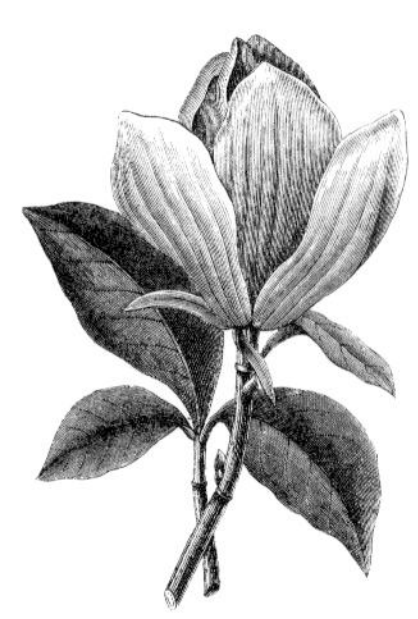

Sometimes patterns are available with tucks included, but they are often not available for the garment you want to make, or are very cumbersome and difficult to understand. What we offer you is a simple method to add tucks to any pattern you find or have. Whether a camisole, a woman's blouse or skirt, or, as we chose, a little boy's shirt, this method is simple and involves a minimum of marking.

Materials needed:

Pattern for boy's shirt
Shirting fabric as required in pattern, plus 1/2 yard extra
Regular sewing thread to match fabric
Sewing machine with a straight stitch

1. Because we are adding pintucks, you will not necessarily be able to follow your pattern layout exactly. Be sure you lay out all your pieces before you start cutting. All pieces except the front will be laid out and cut as per your pattern instructions. The fronts need extra fabric to accommodate the tucks, and the actual shirt front will be cut out after we stitch the tucks. To achieve this, follow our diagram and position the shirt pattern as shown on the fabric, allowing 1" extra for each tuck, and a little extra for good measure. Make snip marks into the fabric indicating the pattern fold lines and the center front line.

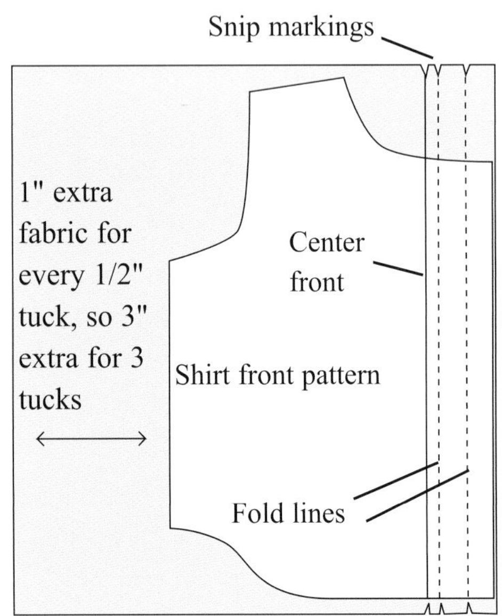

2. Measuring from the center front line, mark the first tuck with a snip mark, 1-1/2" over as shown, and then again every 2". We did three tucks on each front. Make these same marks on the bottom and top as shown. Press a crease, connecting the bottom and top snips.

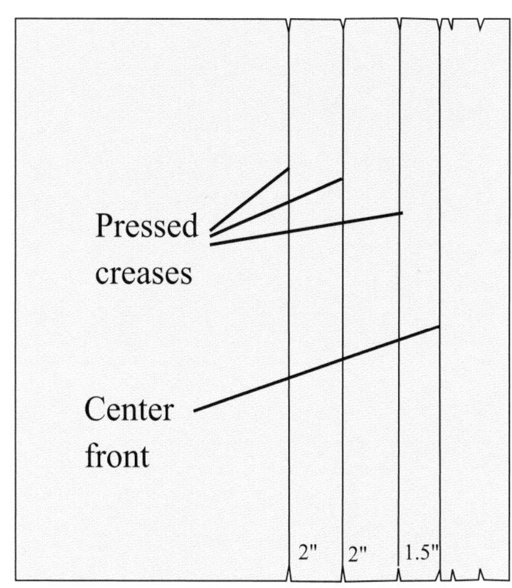

3. Our pintucks are based on a width of 1/2". They could be wider or narrower. The width is measured from the needle to a "spot" on your needle plate or the edge of your presser foot. This may be a 1/2" engraved mark, or you may need to establish it and mark it by measuring from the needle and using masking tape. If you have a machine with variable needle positions, you can move your needle to the correct position to achieve 1/2" from the edge of the presser foot. Fold the fabric on the line you pressed, and using a straight stitch and matching thread, stitch the pintuck in place 1/2" from the folded edge.

> Pintucks were one of the first embellishments to be stitched by hand. These tucking attachments were common attachments on treadle sewing machines. They kept the width of the tuck even as you sewed, even way back then!

3. Stitch the second and third tucks the same and repeat for the other side.

4. We will cut each front separately, insuring that we get one left and one right! With the pattern piece right side up, lay the shirt pattern piece on top of your tucked fabric. Match the center front line and fold lines with your snip marks. Pin in place and cut out one front. Turn the pattern piece over and repeat for the other side.

5. Follow the pattern directions to finish the remainder of the shirt.

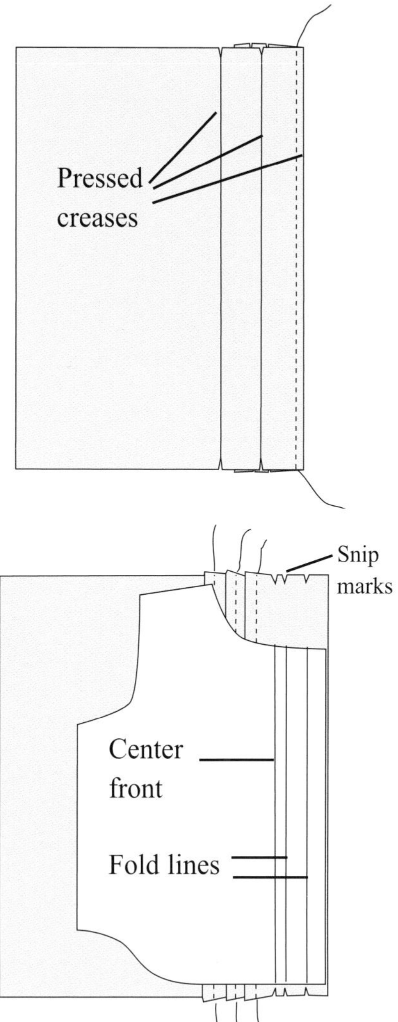

Quick Project

To try out the tucks, or use up your leftovers, make some pot holders. The tucked fabric is ideal, as it has a nice body to help insulate against the hot pans.

Materials needed:

- Cotton fabric scraps
- Cotton batting scraps
- Regular sewing thread to match fabric
- Sewing machine with a straight stitch

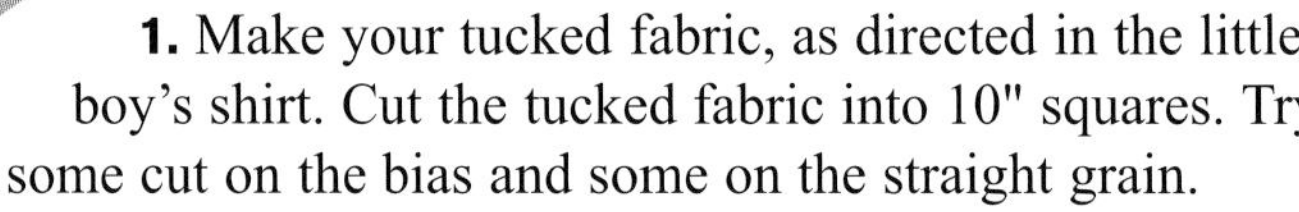

1. Make your tucked fabric, as directed in the little boy's shirt. Cut the tucked fabric into 10" squares. Try some cut on the bias and some on the straight grain.

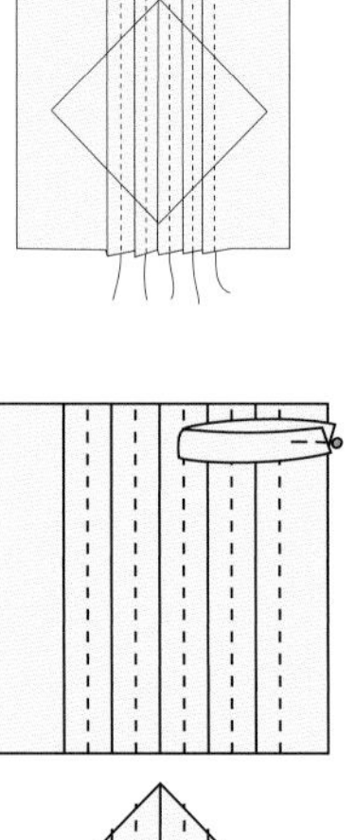

2. Cut a 10" square of plain fabric for each potholder, a 4" x 2" strip of plain fabric for each one, and three 10" squares of cotton batting for each one.

3. Make the hanging loop: Fold the 4" x 2" strip right sides together, creating a 1" x 4" strip. Stitch using a 1/4" seam allowance. Turn right side out.

4. Place the hanging loop in one corner, matching the raw edges. Pin in place.

5. Place the tucked square right sides together with the plain square. Place them on top of the three batting squares. Stitch, using a 1/4" seam allowance, leaving a 3" hole to turn. Clip the corners and turn. Close the hole with a bit of Stitch Witchery, or hand sew shut. Topstitch 1/4" from the edge.

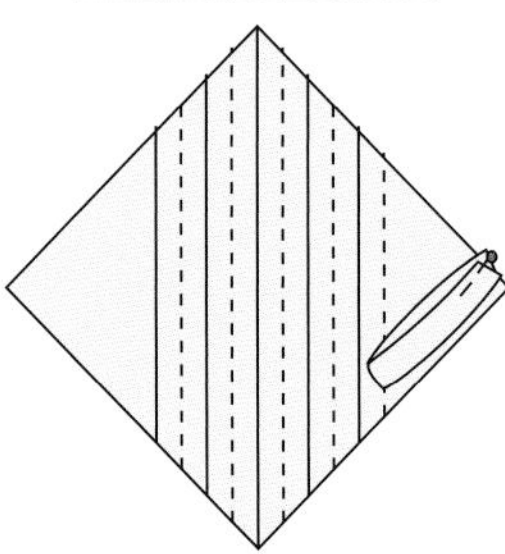

Flip Flop
Oversewn Tucks

Flip flop tucks are traditional tucks, sewn as we did in our little boy's shirt, then oversewn with additional rows of stitching sewn in the opposite direction to anchor them in place. This is a fairly "weighty" technique and is best done with a fairly light-weight fabric, and sewn on a yoke or in an area where additional weight will not affect the garment. We chose a silk broadcloth and embellished the yoke area of our shirt. The results are stunning and add a very sophisticated touch, which is very subtle due to the tone-on-tone texture.

Materials needed:

Shirt pattern with a separate yoke
Shirting fabric of your choice, as called for on the pattern plus 1/2 yard extra
Matching regular sewing thread
Sewing machine with a straight stitch

1. Begin by laying your shirt pattern pieces out on your fabric, and cutting it out according to the pattern instructions. Even though we will be creating fabric for the yoke, you still want to cut out the two yoke pieces as directed; one will be for lining and the other we will use as underlining.

2. Using the extra 1/2 yard of fabric, measure your yoke piece and add 2" extra width and double the length.

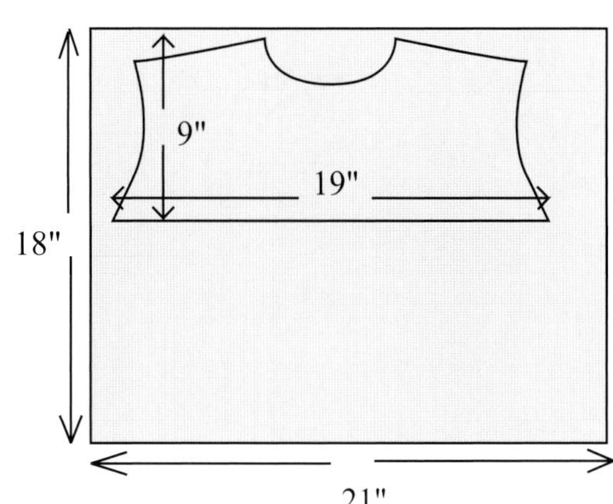

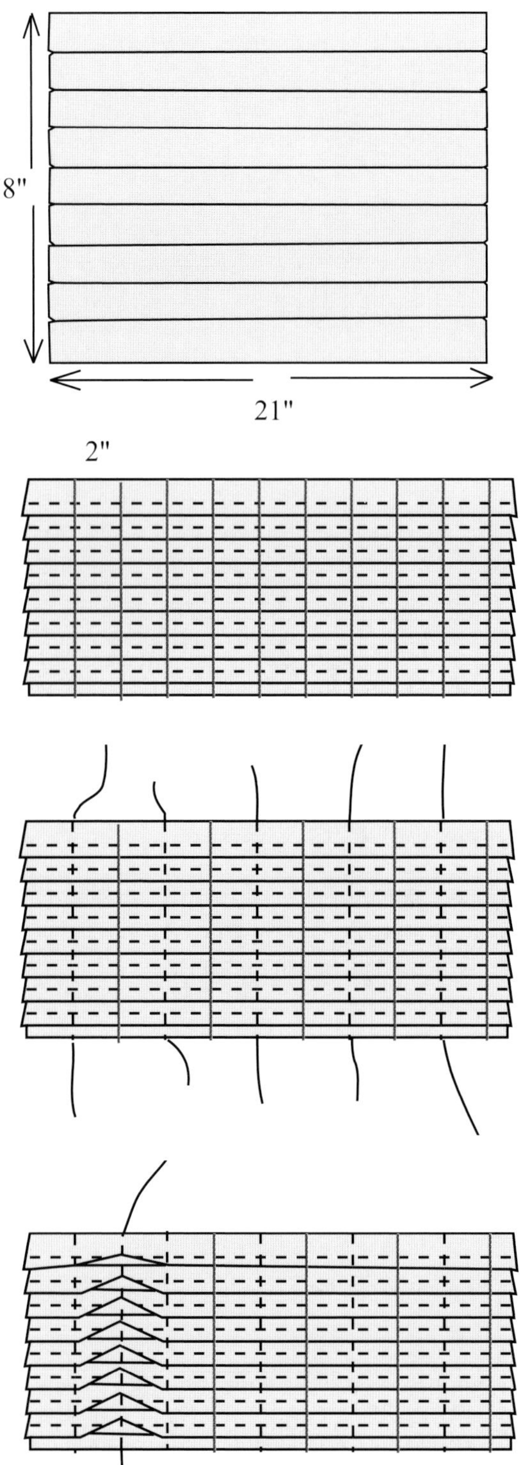

3. Make snip marks 2" apart, on the sides, and press creases connecting these marks.

4. Using a 1/2" seam allowance, stitch the tucks in place. (See pages 52-53 for details). Press.
5. Using an air soluble marker, draw lines 2" apart as shown.

6. Stitch on every other line in the direction the tucks were pressed.

7. Push the tuck in the opposite direction and stitch on the "in-between" lines.

8. When you are done, lay it flat on the ironing board and steam above it. Lay one of the yokes you cut on the back of the tucked fabric. Center it and pin it in place. Straight stitch, following the yoke shape, near the edge. Trim the excess tucked fabric away. This is now your outer yoke. Construct your shirt, following pattern directions.

Book Cover

Whether you put it on a sketch book, an address book or a photo album, our flip flop tucked cover will turn any book into a "coffee table" book!

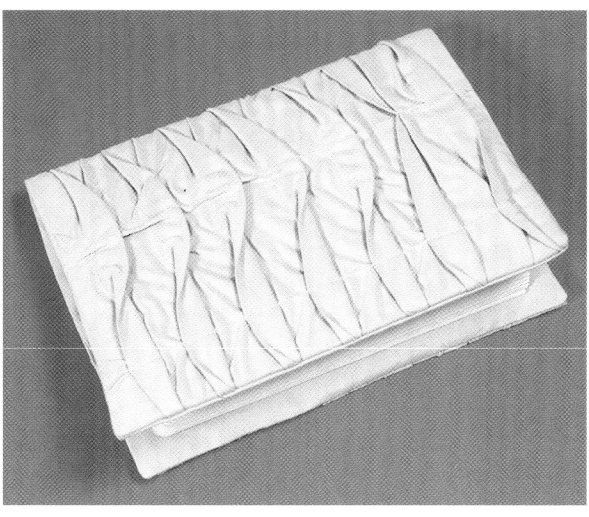

Materials needed:

Book to be covered
Fabric scraps
Heavy weight fusible interfacing
Tape measure
Sewing machine with a straight stitch

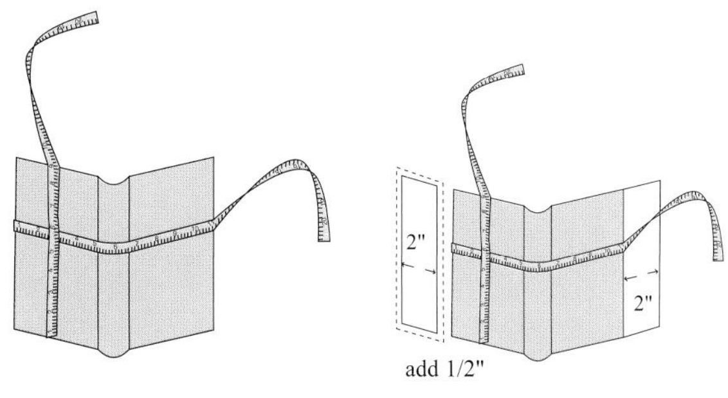

1. Using a tape measure, measure around your book, from edge to edge as shown.

2. Add 1/2" seam allowances on each side, and this is your base pattern. Cut (1) from interfacing and (1) from plain fabric.

3. Create sufficient flip flop tucked fabric to cut one of your base pattern. Fuse the interfacing to the wrong side.

4. Cut from fabric, (2) side pieces, 2" x the height of the book plus 1/2" seam allowances on all sides, as shown. Cut (2) pieces the same from interfacing. Fuse the interfacing to the fabric.

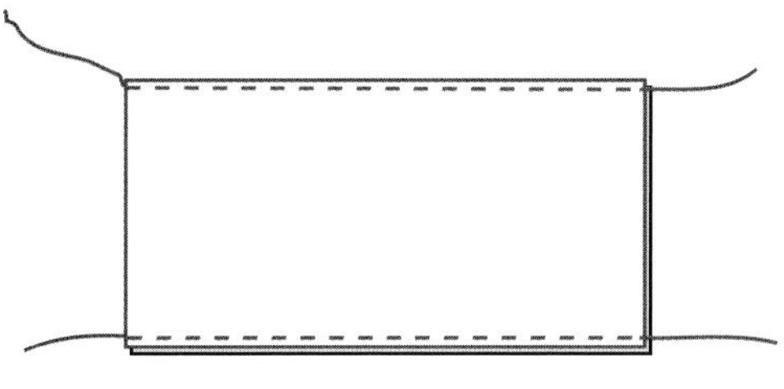

5. Place the interfaced tucked fabric right sides together with the plain fabric piece and sew the top and bottom only, using a 1/4" seam allowance. Turn and press.

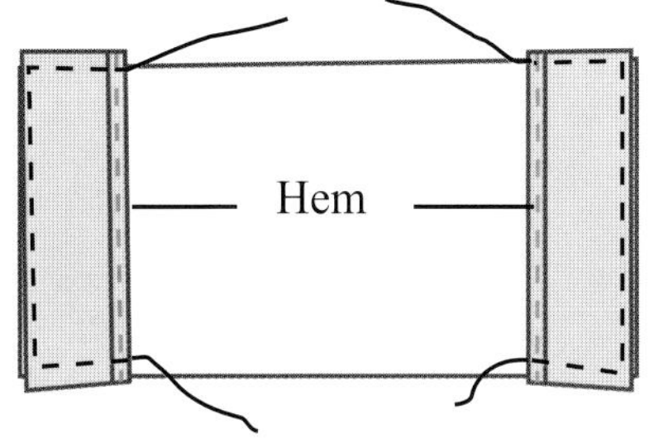

6. Hem one long side of each side piece. Place it right sides together and stitch one side piece on each side of the cover as shown, using 1/4" seam allowance. Turn and press.

Hemstitching

Hemstitching has been popular through the years as a tone-on-tone decoration for blouses, dresses, sheets, pillowcases, hand towels and table linens. Hand hemstitching is created by pulling groups of threads to create a gap, and counting the remaining threads and gathering them into "bunches." In the early part of the century, industrial hemstitchings were popular. They were purchased by the dry goods stores or dry cleaners in the neighborhood, and the customer brought in their garment or yardage to be hemstitched. These machines are rather intimidating, with two bobbins and bobbin cases, and two needles, as well as four spreaders, which are like little fingers which penetrate the fabric, spread out to form a hole, and hold the hole open while the stitch is formed. These machines are still in use today and used to create the garments you purchase ready-made, which contain hemstitching. Another popular use of hemstitching over the years was to create a "picot" edge. The edge of the fabric was hemstitched, and the resulting holes were used to "hook" into to hand crochet an edge.

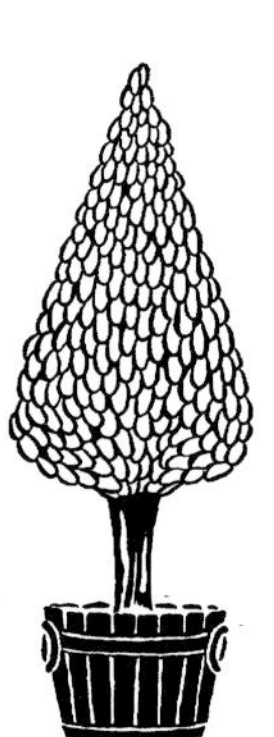

Hemstitching is also used to create an important trim used in heirloom stitching called Entredeaux. The word means "between two" and in this context refers to a trim inserted between two pieces of fabrics, trim or laces. We will show you how to create your own Entredeaux on your sewing machine.

Entredeaux

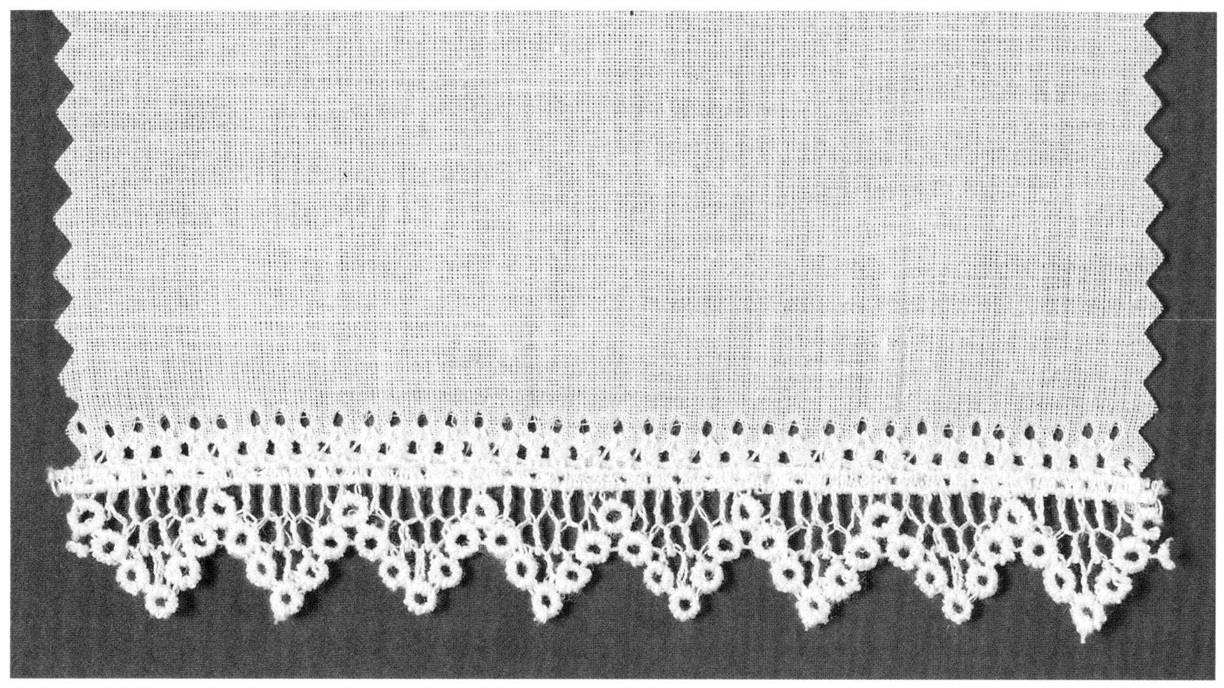

When stitching on light-weight fabrics such as batiste, it is important to stabilize the fabric with spray starch and press it. Do this several times until the fabric is nice and crisp. If an additional stabilizer is needed, a water soluble one such as Solvy is the best, as the tear away or cut away type will fill in the holes we are going to create and show through the sheer fabrics.

Materials needed:

Wing needle
60 wt cotton thread
2" wide strips of batiste, or lace and the garment it is going on
Sewing machine with "hem stitches." See Chart

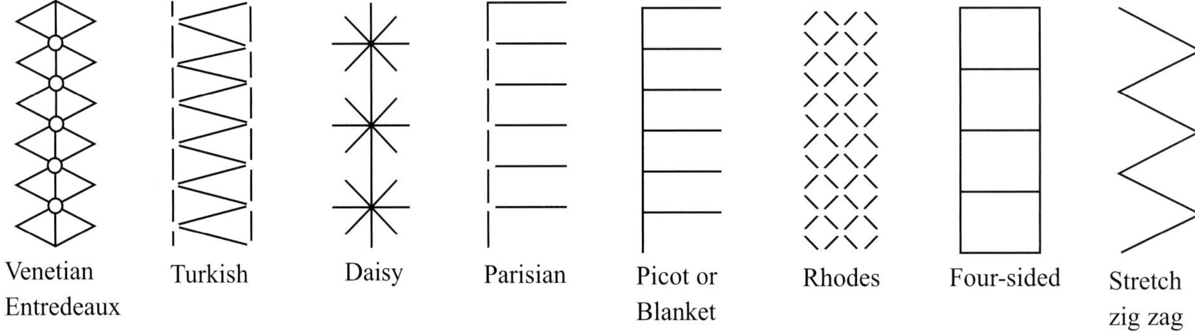

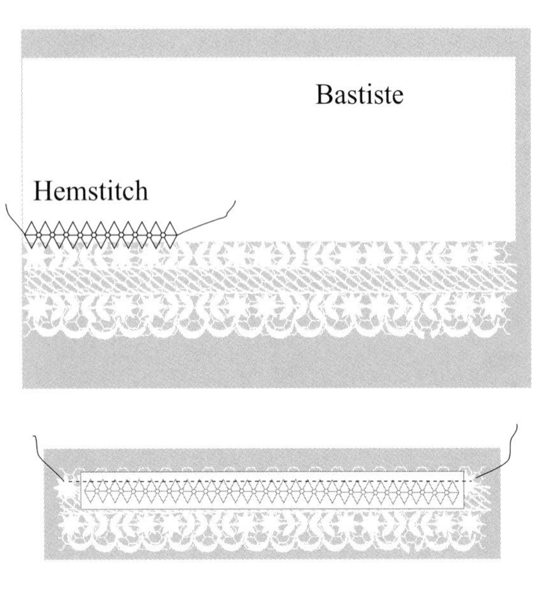

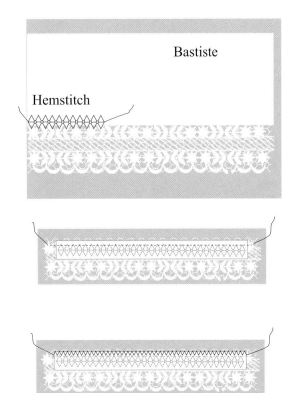

1. Entredeaux can be made separately and then sewn to the lace, or it can be used to attach the lace and sew the Entredeaux in one step. Place the wing needle in the machine. Thread the machine with 60 wt. cotton thread in the bobbin and on top. Usually there is no need to adjust the tension. Test the stitches you have chosen on a scrap. The holes created should be crisp and clean. If they are not, check your owner's manual to see if you have a balance adjustment. As a hem stitch is formed, it goes in and out of the same hole a number of times. If the balance is not adjusted correctly, it misses by a thread, and the hold is "fuzzy." The balance control, if available, fine tunes the stitch. Don't sew too fast, and if some puckering occurs, try pressing it before you go any further; that usually takes care of any puckers that occur. If not, try loosening the upper tension by one number.

2. When you are satisfied with the stitch, you can stitch separate Entredeaux on 2" wide strips of muslin or you can place your lace on the garment itself, as we did, and stitch the Entredeaux so the bulk of the stitch is on the batiste and just catches the edge of the lace.

3. If separate strips of Entredeaux are sewn, place them right sides together with the lace, and straight stitch.

4. Then for durability, stitch a small zig zag, 1.5 width and 1.5 length, next to the row of straight stitching.

Hemstitched
Placemats and Napkins

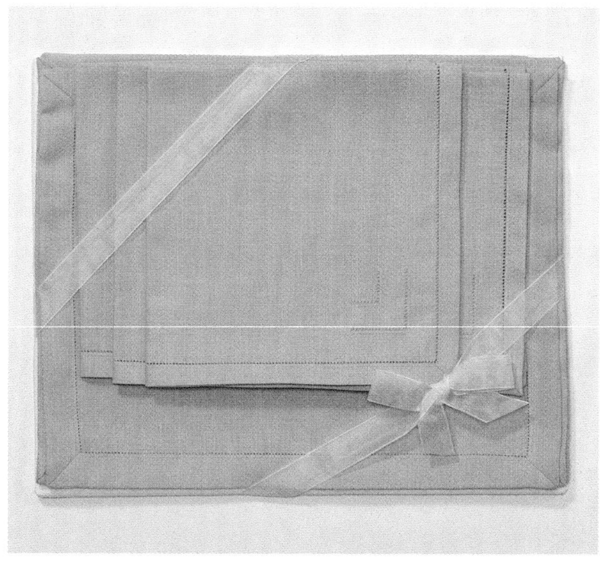

Natural fibers such as linen, linen/cotton blend or cotton are best for hemstitching. We are pushing the fibers of the fabric to one side, and trying to convince them to stay there. Natural fibers will be much more cooperative. Synthetics tend to have a memory and resist being re-configured! On the other hand, if you prefer the easy care of blends, go for a cotton blend with as high a cotton content as possible.

The amount of fabric needed will depend on the width, which can vary from 36" to 60". Our measurements are approximate, depending on the width of your fabric, and whether you want generously sized dinner napkins, or luncheon proportions. The range for napkins is usually between 15" and 20" square, finished. We used a 20" finished size. To our 20", we added (4) "hem widths." We did a wide generous hem of 3/4". Because it is turned up twice, that equals 1-1/2" on each side; hence, (4) hem widths or 3". If you turn up a 1/4" hem, you would need to add 1" extra (1/4" times 4). You may be able to cut a napkin next to a placemat or do all napkins side by side and placemats side by side.

Our finished placemats measure 22" x 16". Following the same formula as the napkins, we wanted a 1" hem, so we cut them 18" x 24". Cut a sample test piece and do all the steps on the test as well as on your napkins.

Materials needed: Fabric for napkins and placemats, as described above
Fine 60 wt cotton thread to match
Wing needle, size 100 or 120

1. The first step in our napkins and placemats is to miter the corners. Following the directions, miter all the corners.

Mitered Corners: *A mitered corner is desirable to reduce the bulk in the corner area of a hem.*

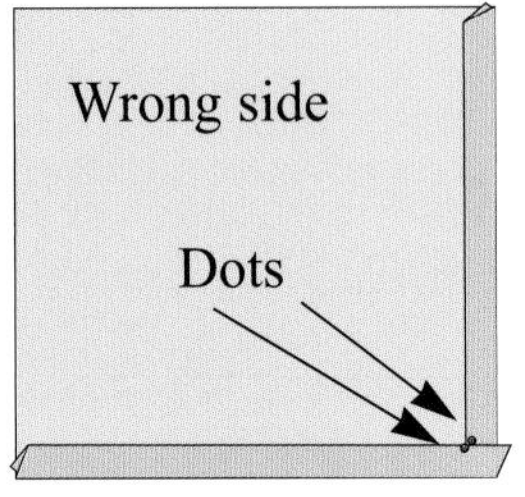

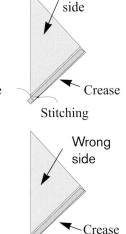

1. To stitch a mitered corner, begin by pressing the hem in place. This is usually done by pressing the width of the hem to the wrong side once, and then folding over to press the same amount over again. For our dinner napkins, we pressed 1" and then 1" again. The amount will vary with the scale of your project, from as little as 1/4", to 2" each time for some placemats. Mark a dot, using an air soluble marker where the corners intersect, as shown.

Wrong side

Unfold so edge is folded over one time only

Crease

Dots

2. Unfold one time on each side so the hem is folded one time only.

3. Fold as shown, so your two dots meet. Stitch from the dots to the point where the crease lines intersect. Be sure to backstitch at the beginning and end.

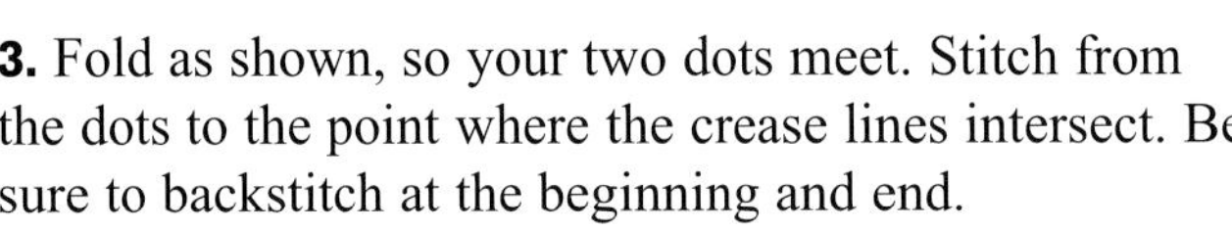

Wrong side

Crease

Stitching

4. Trim away the excess fabric from the corner as shown.

5. Turn and press.

Wrong side

Mitered corner

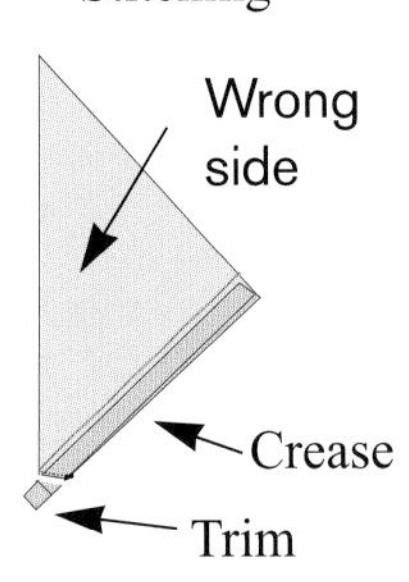

2. Just at the edge of the hem, we will now pull a couple threads. This step is optional, but does accentuate the "holes" and make them bigger.

3. This step is optional, but makes your hemstitching go smoother. Straight stitch your hem in place, sewing as close to the edge of the fold as possible. On your sample, test your hemstitching without straight stitching first, and with straight stitching first, to determine if it is necessary for the stitch you have chosen.

4. Now place the wing needle into your sewing machine. Use the fine thread in both the bobbin and on top. Check your instruction manual for suggestions of stitches on your individual sewing machine. The chart on page 60 shows you some universal possibilities. Technically a hemstitch is one that goes back and forth in the hole more than one time. Some stitches may work very well, even though they aren't intended for hemstitching. Try varying the length and width of the stitch for different effects.

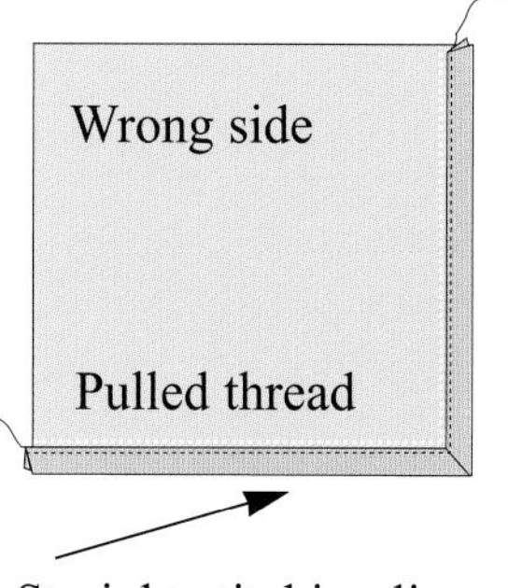

Straight stitching line

5. On our napkins and placemats, we used the hemstitch that resembles the blanket stitch, at a 3" width and 3" length. The straight stitch portion of the stitch rides in the line of pulled threads, and the stitch that jumps to the side catches the folded edge of the hem.

6. We added detail in the corner of each napkin, 1" in from the edge, as described below in the cocktail napkins.

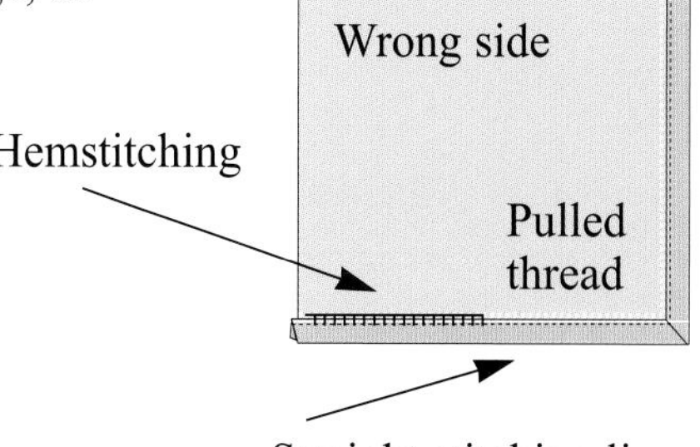

Straight stitching line

Quick Project

Cocktail Napkins

Great to use up scraps and take along as a hostess gift! Stitch up a few of these to put by the hors d'oeuvres and get ready for the compliments!

Follow the directions for the regular napkins, turning up a 1" hem. When done, measure 1/2" in from the edge and mark as shown. The first is 1/2" and the inner one is 1". Carefully snip the threads at the starting point, and pull several threads from the marked area. Hemstitch as before.

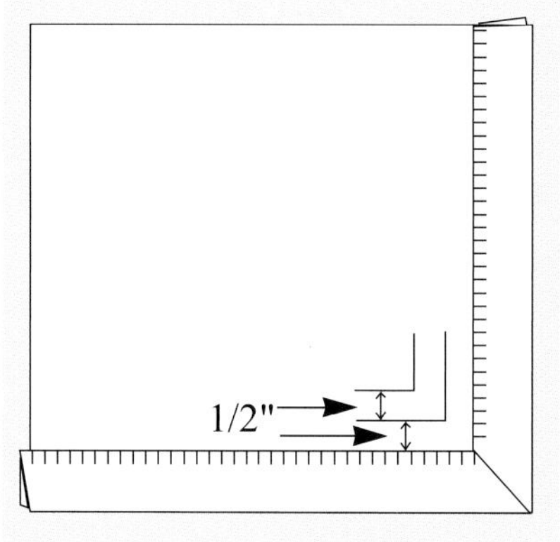

Materials needed:

12" square of linen for each napkin
Fine 60 wt cotton thread to match
Wing needle, size 100 or 120

Drawn Thread Work

Materials needed:

Even weave linen-like fabric:
Measure window and allow 1-1/2 times the width and the length, plus 10"
Fine 60 wt. cotton thread to match
Serger tweezers
Open toe appliqué foot or button sew on foot
Sewing machine with a zig zag stitch

1. Pull threads and square up the fabric on all four sides. Cut the fabric in half to make two curtain halves.

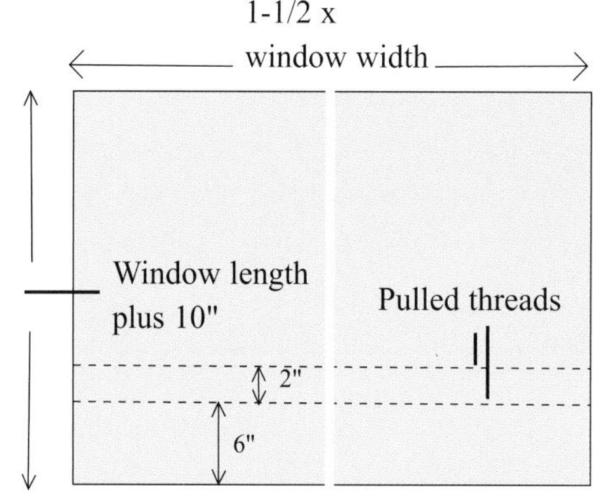

2. Thread your sewing machine and bobbin with 60 wt. cotton thread to match the fabric.

3. Measure up 6" from the bottom, and pull a thread at that point. Pull approximately 6 more threads, depending on the coarseness of your fabric. The open space should be about 1/2". Measure up 2" and repeat as shown.

4. Select a zig zag, 2" width and 2" length. Fold the bottom raw edge up to meet the first row of pulled threads. Press. Stitch hem in place with zig zag.

5. Fold side hems in 1/2" and again 1/2". Press. Zig zag in place.

6. On top edge, press under 1/2". Fold down 3-1/2". Using a straight stitch, stitch along the bottom of the folded hem edge. Stitch again 1" from the top fold.

7. Set your sewing machine for a zig zag, 4 width. Drop or cover the feed teeth. The length setting doesn't matter because when you drop the feed teeth, the length is disconnected.

8. Place the open toe appliqué foot or the button sew on foot on your sewing machine. Starting at the edge of the curtain, in the area that you pulled the threads, place the fabric under the presser foot. Using the serger tweezers, gather a set number of threads together; we used the number 7. Being careful not to hit the tweezers with the needle, stitch over these gathered up threads about 10 full zig zags.

9. Using the tweezers, gather the next 7 threads into a bunch. Lift presser foot, and move to the next bunch of threads. Stitch as before.

10. Continue across the curtain. Repeat for the second row.

Quick Project

Bookmark

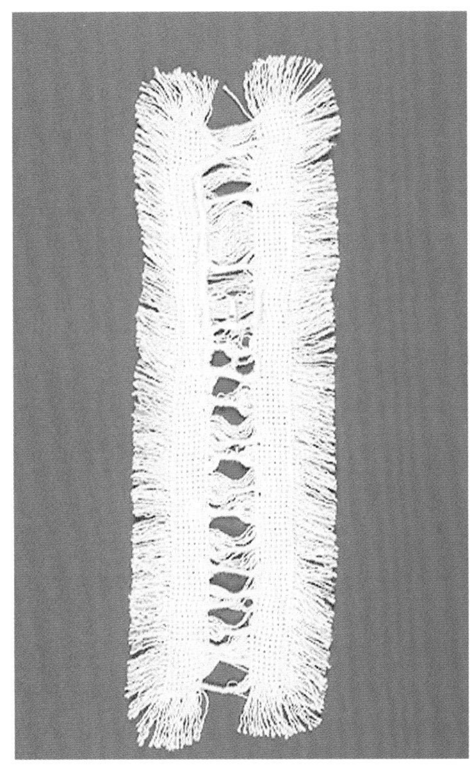

Using scraps from your curtain or any other even weave, loosely woven fabric, make bookmarks for the readers in your circle of family and friends. It's a great incentive for young readers to have a personalized bookmark of their own.

Materials needed:

3" by 10" linen or linen-like fabric.
Matching or contrasting thread
Open toe appliqué foot

1. Using an air-soluble marker, draw the name on the fabric, about 3/4" high, as shown.

2. Set your sewing machine for a small zig zag, 2" width and 2" length. Stitch all around the book mark 1/2" in from the edge. This will be the guide for fringing the edges when we are done.

3. Pull out the threads in the lengthwise direction in the middle section. Leave an open area about 3/4".

4. Set your machine for a satin stitch, 4" width, 1/2" length. Use the open toe appliqué foot for better vision. Following the lines drawn, stitch over the letters, forming the name. Stitch randomly on the remaining threads to form an abstract design.

5. Fringe the edges, up to the stitched line.

Appliqué

Appliqué or "applied work" is the method of applying one fabric to another, usually by means of a decorative stitch. There are three main forms: "onlay," laying one fabric on top of another; "reverse," cutting away the uppermost fabric to reveal the fabric below it; and "inlay," cutting the same motif from each of two fabrics, and laying the contrasting one in place in the resulting hole.

It was probably first seen in the work of Persians or Indians as an imitation of the rich embroideries. It has appeared and reappeared throughout the centuries—used lavishly by the Egyptians and Greeks, appearing later during the crusades as a decoration on knights' surcoats, horse trappings etc., and later for use in church banners. Mola appliqué, a form of reverse appliqué, is associated with the Cuna women of Panama and Columbia. Modern designs do not confine themselves to ordinary fabrics, but avail themselves of braids, leathers, felt, Ultrasuede and much more.

Shadow appliqué, or shadow work, is a type of appliqué where a sheer overlay fabric is placed over cut designs, and decorative stitches are used to hold the two layers together. The resulting shapes show through as a darker shadow. This is usually done white on white, but can also be seen using a color underneath. Original shadow embroidery was worked with thread alone on a single layer of fabric. The bulk of the thread lay on the back of the fabric, with only a few edging stitches appearing on the front. The threads on the back side of the fabric showed through, resulting in a shadowed effect.

Designs for appliqué are all around us. There are a wide variety of patterns available just for appliqué, but there are also unending supplies available in children's coloring books, clip art, greeting cards and greeting paper; one favorite actually came off a brown paper grocery sack. It was a beautiful Cornucopia design. Look for bold, rather simple, designs without fussy details.

Appliqué work can be worked strictly for decorative purposes, or it can be used to hide a stain or unwanted rip in a garment.

Hand Appliqué by Machine -

Baltimore Album Pillow

Our first appliqué project is done with a technique called hand appliqué by machine. Originally, it was done by hand, utilizing the blind stitch, so the stitches didn't show. It is a favorite quilting technique, often used in the Baltimore Album designs. We've supplied the actual size patterns for your pillow. If you want to go on and do full quilts, any patterns designed to be stitched by hand are suitable for you to adapt to machine sewing. We utilize invisible thread so you don't see the stitches.

Materials needed:

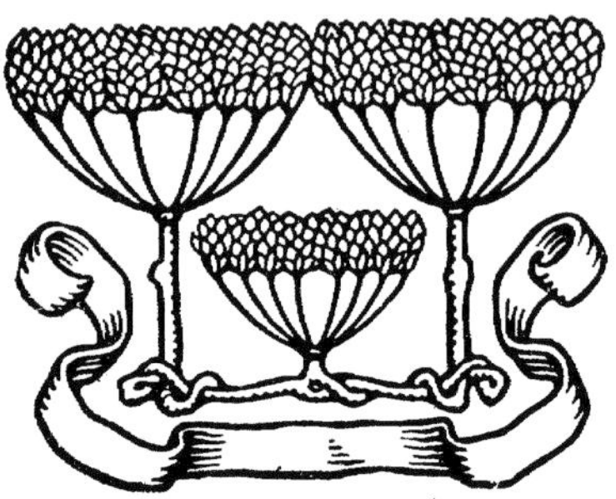

Sewing machine with zig zag or blanket stitch
1-1/4 yard of white 100% cotton Muslin
1/8 yard each, tone on tone 100% cotton prints,
green, yellow, red and purple
1/4 yard light-weight fusible interfacing
Smoke colored invisible thread
Regular weight white sewing thread
Glue stick or other temporary basting glue
Pinking shears
Open toe appliqué foot
20" round pillow form or polyfil
Optional - rolled hem foot
Optional - gathering foot

1. Using the full-size patterns provided, trace off the following of each shape onto your interfacing. A pencil or ball-point pen is fine for tracing. As you trace, be sure the "glue" side (the bumpy side) is up, and be sure to leave at least 1/2" between each piece for seam allowances.

Trace: (9) circles for yellow centers
(9) flowers
(27) circles for Purple berries
(36) leaves

2. Cut apart the above "categories" and put the 9 yellow center circles on the yellow fabric, the 9 flower shapes on the red fabric, the 27 circles on the purple fabric and the 36 leaves on the green fabric. The colored fabric should be right side up, with the interfacing laid on top glue (bumpy) side up. DO NOT CUT OUT THE ACTUAL SHAPES.

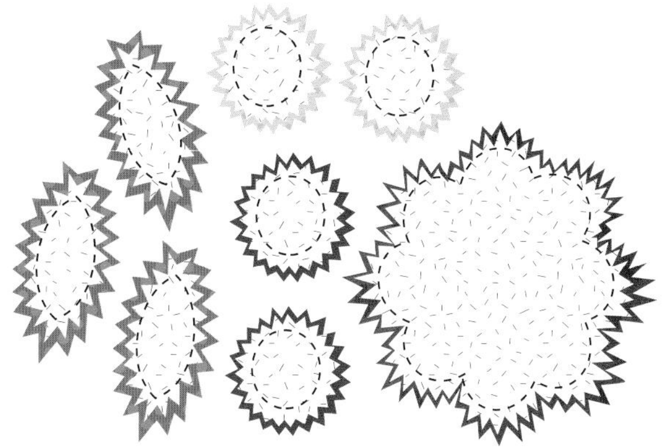

3. Stitch on the drawn lines, using a short straight stitch.

4. Cut out the shapes with your pinking shears.

5. Cut a small slit in the interfacing, and turn right side out. Carefully press to adhere the interfacing

6. Trace off the pattern design four times. The pattern is 1/4 of the circle. Tape your four traced patterns together to form a full circle. Lay the single motif in the center. Lay the pattern under your white fabric. You should be able to see the design through the fabric. Then, put your appliqué shapes in place, and glue them down with a glue stick, or pin them in place.

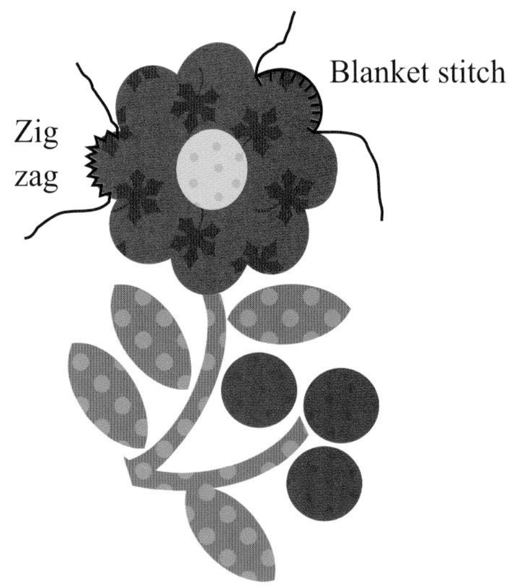

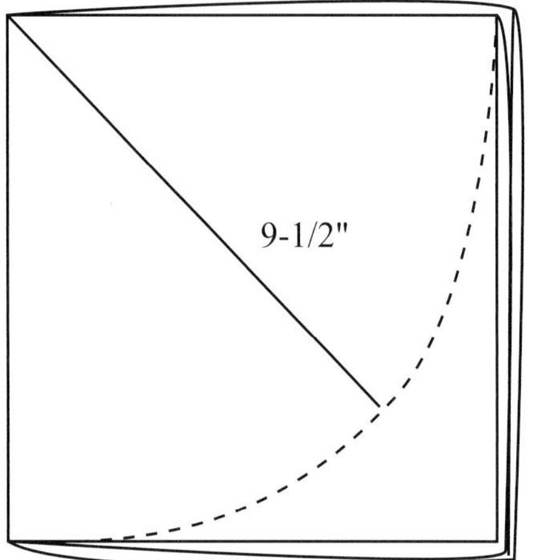

7. Thread your machine with invisible thread on top and regular white sewing thread in the bobbin. Experiment on scraps to determine the correct tension. You probably need to lower the top tension 1 or 2 numbers. Lower it until you don't see any white bobbin thread on top. Choose a small zig zag, 1.5 width and 1.5 length, or a small blanket stitch. The stitches should just barely go on and off the appliqué.

8. Now we are ready to make the pillow. Cut (4) ruffle strips, 4" wide x 44" long. Fold your appliquéd design in quarters, carefully. Pin through all layers, so it won't shift. Measure from the folded corner 9-1/2" out, as shown.

9. Cut out your circle following the marked lines. Using this as your pattern, cut a matching back.

10. We will hem the ruffle strips, using a rolled hem foot. If you don't have this foot, you can hem without it but it's harder. By hemming the strips before we sew them together, we eliminate the problem of the seam going through the hemmer foot. After they are hemmed, stitch them end to end to form a circle. We used a French seam by stitching them first wrong sides together, trimming to 1/8" and then stitching the right sides together, enclosing the raw edges.

11. Gather the ruffle, using your gathering foot, or by running two rows of long straight stitch and hand pulling the gathers. The gathering foot is much quicker and much more even. Pin the ruffle in place on the appliquéd portion of the pillow, and stitch it in place. Place the pillow back right sides together, and stitch, leaving a 6" opening to turn. Turn right sides out and insert the pillow form or polyfil. Hand stitch the opening closed.

Actual pattern size

Quick Project

Mini Baltimore Album Pillow

Whether it's used for a favorite doll, as a pin cushion, or filled with your favorite potpourri, a mini pillow is a great way to practice the technique or use up scraps. Follow the above directions with one motif. Our circle measures 5" across.

Blanket Stitched Hand Appliqué by Machine -

Child's Polarfleece Jacket

Our next appliqué project utilizes the same fusible interfacing methods we used in the Baltimore Album pillow, in addition to Ultrasuede. The difference is that we are going to use a blanket stitch with decorative stitching to stitch down the designs. The blanket stitching adds a nice outline, defining the details of the design. Choose a jacket pattern that is simple in nature, without complicated yokes, darts, collars, etc.

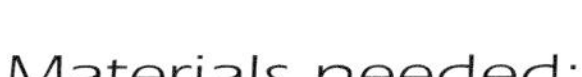

Materials needed:

Sewing machine with blanket stitch or blind hem stitch
Jacket pattern of your choice
Lime green Polarfleece as called for in the pattern
1/4 yard blue ribbing or interlock knit for binding - check your yardage; depending on the ribbing width you need 2" wide strips of sufficient length to go around the jacket edges and sleeves.
Variety of colorful scraps of tone on tone cotton fabrics and Ultrasuede
Regular sewing thread: lime green
Cotton embroidery thread: bright colors to match your fabric scraps
1/4" to 1/2" wide grosgrain ribbon scraps, bright colors
1/4 yard light weight fusible interfacing
Fabric glue stick or pins
Pinking shears
Open toe appliqué foot

1. Choose the designs you want to make with the cotton fabrics. Trace them off on the "glue" (bumpy) side of your interfacing, using a pencil or ball-point pen. Leave at least 1/2" between designs. Cut them apart using your pinking shears, but do not cut out the designs. Lay your cotton fabric right side up, with the interfacing on top. Be sure the glue (bumpy) side remains up. Stitch on your drawn lines.

2. Cut out with your pinking shears.

3. Cut a slit in the interfacing and turn right side out. Carefully press to adhere the interfacing.

4. Trace off the remaining shapes to be cut from Ultrasuede onto plain paper and using them as your pattern, cut out the Ultrasuede shapes.

5. Cut out your jacket. Do not cut facings. Only use front, back, sleeve and collar or hood if applicable. Arrange the appliqués on your jacket pieces and glue or pin in place. Place the ribbon now, as it may go behind a bird, and should go under the bird houses to conceal the raw ends of the ribbon.

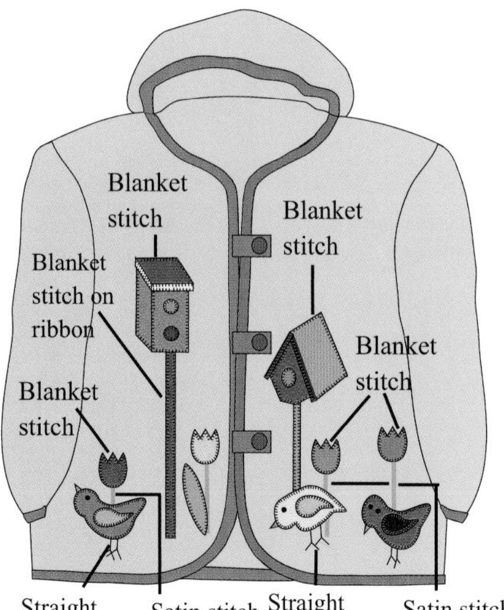

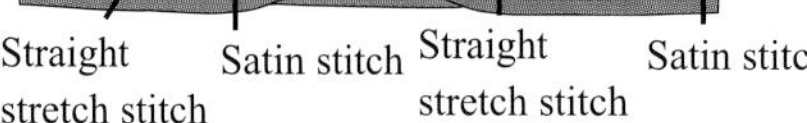

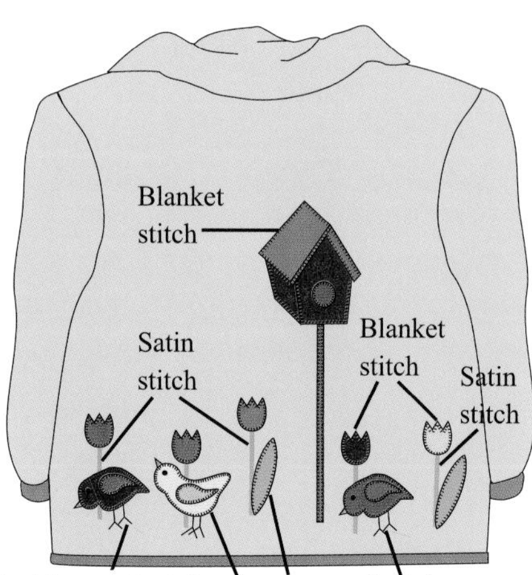

6. Select the blanket stitch or blind hem on your sewing machine. Practice on scraps to get a pleasing stitch size and correct tension. You can use lime green regular sewing thread in the bobbin and the cotton embroidery colors on the top only. Loosen your top tension a bit if you are pulling up bobbin thread to the top.

7. Stitch around your appliqués. Mix and match your thread colors. We used a satin stitch, zig zag, set at 4-6 width and short length, about 1/2, for sewing the stems of the tulips. Place a scrap of stabilizer underneath. See pages 9, 12 and13-14 for more information about threads, sewing machine feet and stabilizers.

Fold

8. To finish your jacket, sew the seams according to pattern directions. Cut your binding strips across the grain so they stretch. They should be cut 2" wide and be of sufficient length to go all the way around the jacket and sleeve bottoms. Trim off any hem allowance on the sleeve bottoms and jacket bottom.

9. Sew the binding strips end to end. Press them in half, lengthwise, wrong sides together.

Wrong side of fabric

Raw edges even

10. Place the raw edges of the binding even with the raw edge of the Polarfleece on the WRONG side of the jacket fabric. Stitch 1/4" from the edge.

11. Fold over to the right side, and stitch in place with the blanket stitch or the blind hem stitch.

12. Make a tube of leftover binding and stitch in place to form closure loops.

Actual size patterns

Blindstitch/decorative

stitch appliqué work

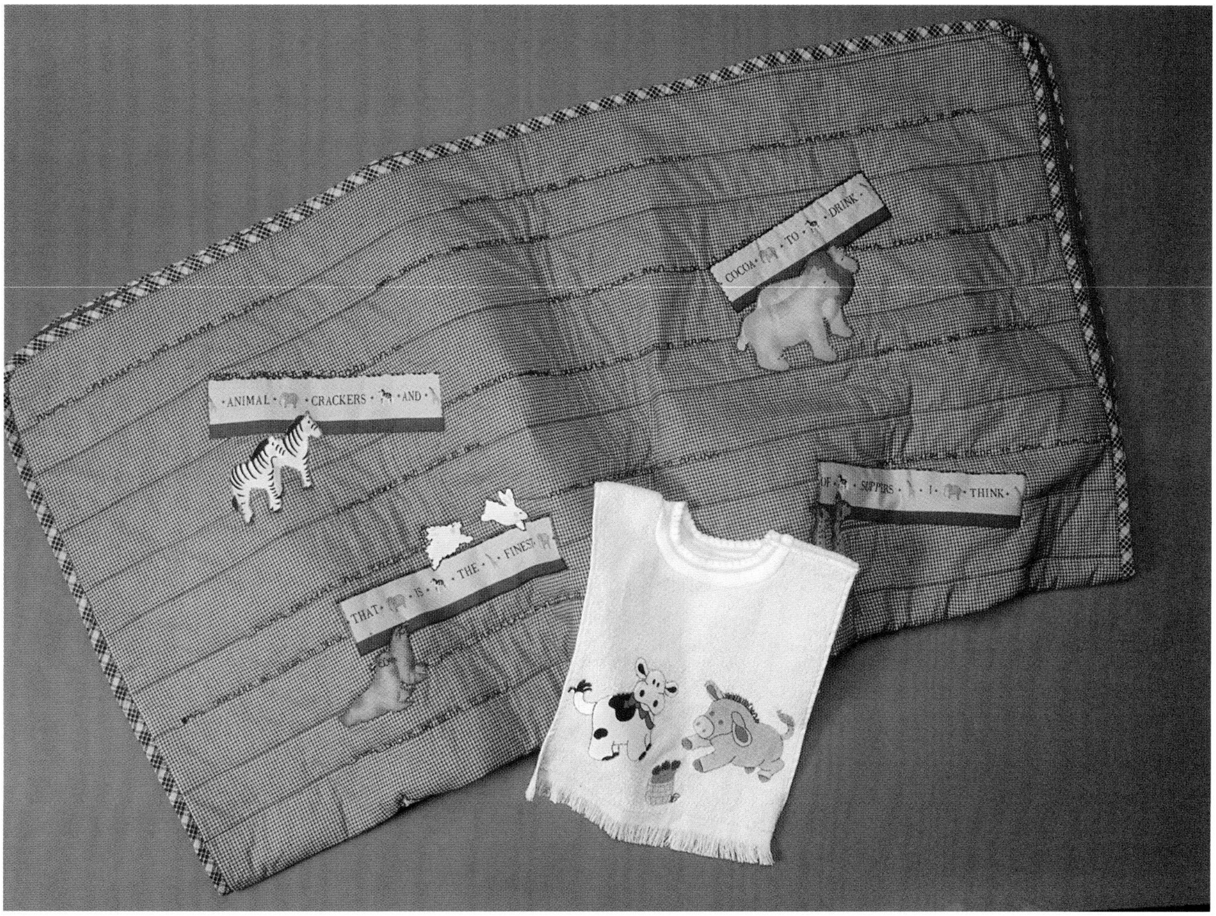

For our appliqué work, we used cutout shapes from existing fabric. In our modern machine world, we also have stabilizers which make the task much faster. Any stitch may be used, from a straight or satin stitch to one of the decorative ones. The important part is covering the edges to prevent fraying and loosening if laundering will be done.

Baby Blanket

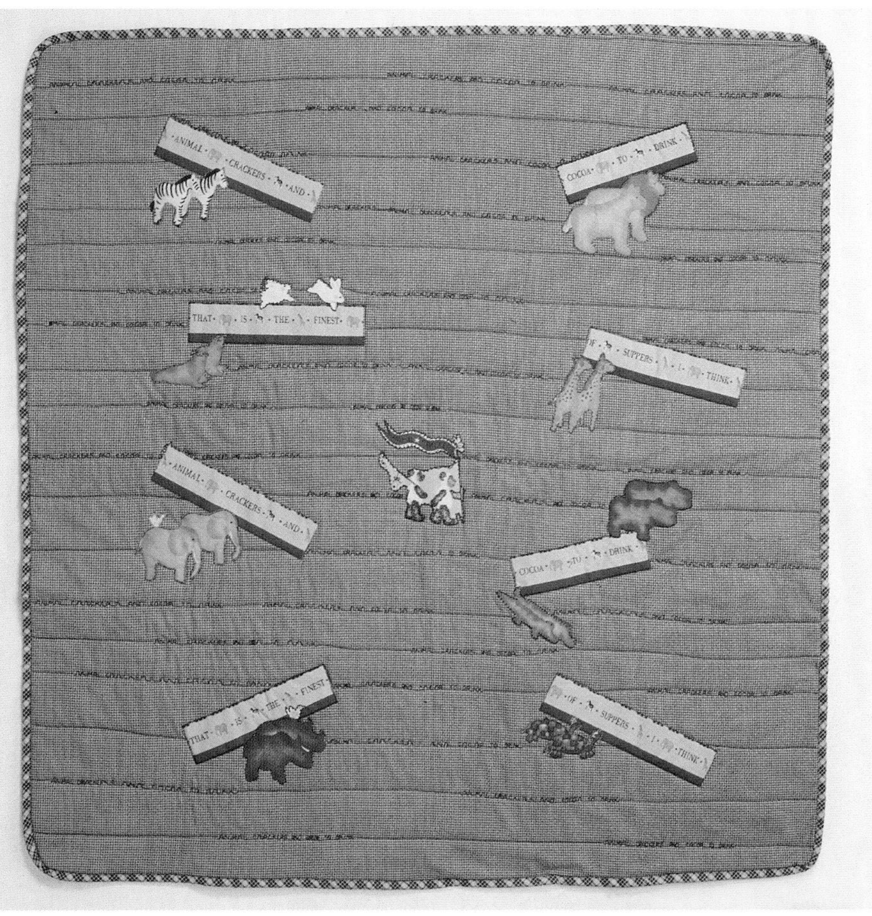

When shopping, we chanced on the "Animal Crackers" appliqué fabric, which happens to be one of the favorite poems from when Betty's children were young. And let's face it: animal crackers are still a very popular snack with the children of today. Then we got the coordinating background fabric. The edge finish fabric was cut from part of the piece the animals and poem were cut from (this piece of fabric was designed to be made into a bumper pad for a crib). We realize you may not be able to find this animal cracker fabric, but any fabric with shapes to cut out is very useable.

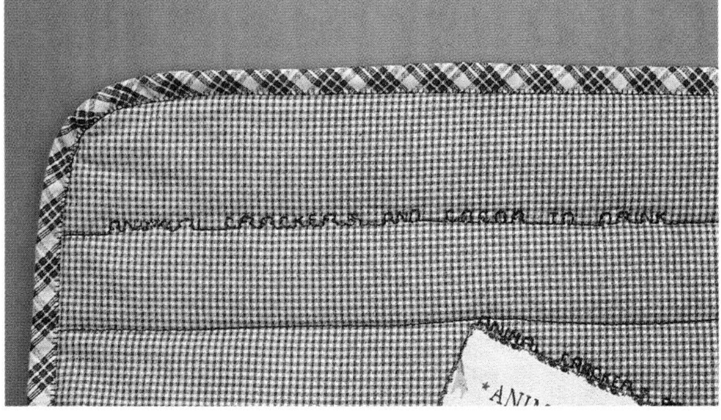

Materials needed:

2-1/2 yards of 45" material
Fabric from which to cut out designs, 1-1/2 yards (depending on pattern)
Crib size batting
Steam-a-Seam II (or other iron-on fusible web)
Megasheen Rayon Embroidery thread - garnet
Sulky Rayon Embroidery 30 wt. thread - navy
Temporary spray adhesive
Appliqué presser foot
Walking foot

1. Straighten cut ends of fabric and cut into two 45" x 45" pieces.

2. Apply Steam-A-Seam II to the back of the motif fabric.

3. Cut out the designs to be appliqués. Remove paper backing.

Stretch blind hem

4. Lay top of quilt base out flat, and arrange appliqué pieces into a pleasing arrangement. (We decided to incorporate parts of the poem without animals.) The Steam-a-Seam II works well, as it has a temporary adhesive that will hold it in place temporarily while the pattern is being arranged. (There are other temporary holds available which we will discuss in another section.)

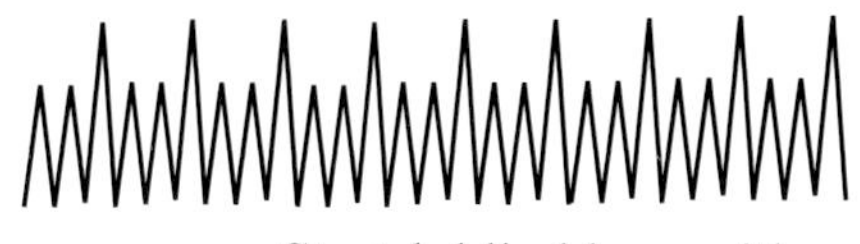

Stretch blind hem with stitch length shortened

5. When a satisfactory arrangement has been achieved, iron appliqués to quilt top. This holds them in place while the stitching is done.

6. We used a stretch blind stitch and a blanket stitch from our machine for the appliqué. We rotated stitches on different pieces. It is possible to use more or less decorative appliqué stitches, and shorten or lengthen the stitch to meet your needs.

7. Begin stitching around the ironed on appliqués with the decorative stitch. It is important to cover the edges of the decorative fabric, both for appearance and stability.

8. When all appliqués are stitched, lay out backing fabric and layer it with batting and blanket top. There are temporary adhesives on the market today to hold the layers together (follow manufacturer's instructions when using). Spray this onto the fabric as you are creating the layers. If a spray adhesive is not available, pin layers to hold them in position as you quilt.

9. Put walking foot on sewing machine. We chose to use a straight stitch and the lettering from our machine as our quilting stitch. This was done in a horizontal strip technique. We started in the center of the quilt and worked to the ends. We did a random pattern and programmed the saying into the computer machine. If you do not have lettering, choose a stitch from your machine and use as the quilting stitch.

Join at 45-degree angle

10. Square edges and trim uneven portions on edges. We rounded our corners also. Straight stitch around these edges with a 1/4" seam. This helps keep all layers together as binding is attached.

11. For edging on blanket, we made our own blanket binding. We cut 2-1/2" strips on the straight grain of the fabric, and angled the ends to 45 degrees. We sewed these ends together and pressed the seams open. Then we pressed this piece vertically into a 1-1/4" wide strip, with *wrong* sides together.

12. Pick the middle of a side to start applying binding, and fold end of strip to inside.

13. With machine set to straight stitch and binding on wrong side of quilt, stitch around edges. You will want to catch at least a quarter inch of binding and blanket. (Where you have stitched around the edges is a good guide). When you have sewn all around the blanket, overlap the starting point so no raw edges show.

14. Press binding to right side of quilt. Pin in place, barely covering previous row of stitching.

15. Stitch in place. We used the blanket stitch and the garnet Megasheen thread.

16. Give as a gift, or use for your own baby dear and enjoy!

Baby Bib

with appliqué designs

Since all older babies and toddlers seem to like animals, these seemed like a logical choice for our bib. This is a quick and easy item to enhance, and whoever has enough bibs! Seems like a clean one is needed for each meal, unless your babies are neater eaters than ours were.

Materials needed:

Baby bib (purchased or made from finger tip towel)
Small piece or scraps of fabric for cutting characters
Steam-a-Seam II (or other stabilizer)
Decorative thread
Bobbin thread
Appliqué presser foot

1. Follow steps 2 and 3 in appliqués for the baby blanket.

2. Arrange stabilized, cut shapes onto bib, and iron appliqués in place.

3. Put appliqué foot on machine, and thread with appropriate threads. Either loosen the upper tension a number, or thread extra tension on bobbin case. (This assures none of the bobbin thread will show on the topside of the finished bib).

4. We stitched with the stretch blind hem stitch on our machine, shortening the stitch length.

5. When finished, press if necessary and bring on dinner!

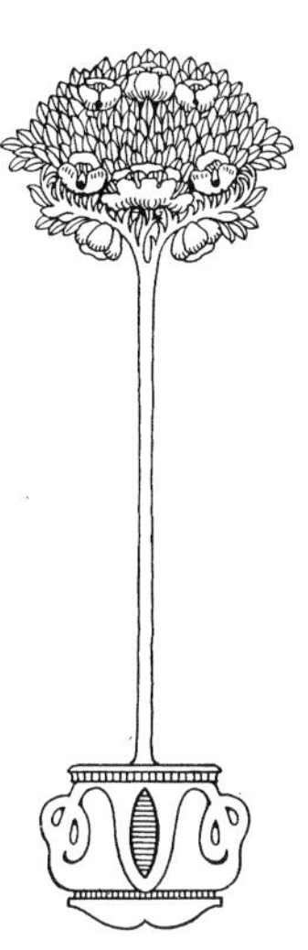

Reverse Appliqué

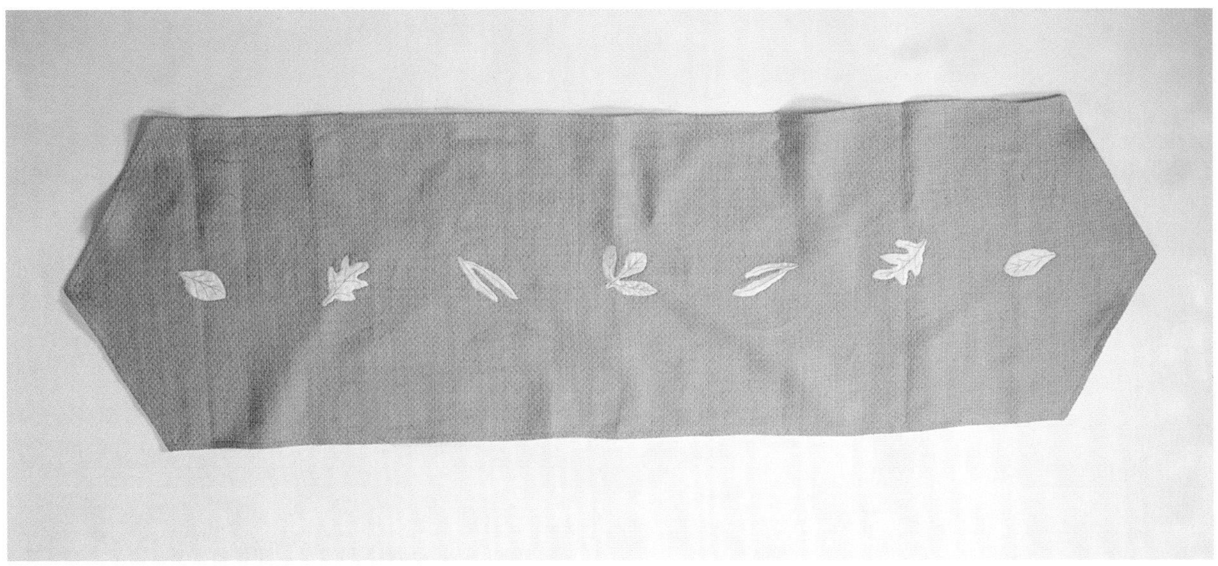

Reverse appliqué is a technique where two or more fabrics are layered, and the top layer is cut to reveal the underneath fabric or fabrics. Mola appliqué, a type of work done by the Cuna women of Panama and Columbia, is a typical example of this technique. Our table runner is made with two fabrics, and the resulting designs are embellished with embroidered details.

Materials needed:

Taupe linen: 1/2 yard 60" or 1-3/4 yard 45"
Muslin: 1/2 yard 60" or 1-3/4 yard 45"
1/4 yard light-weight fusible interfacing
Taupe 60 wt. cotton thread
Regular weight sewing thread
4" x 1/2" strip of fusible web like Stitch Witchery
(Optional) Darning foot or embroidery hoop
(Optional) Open toe appliqué foot

1. Cut both fabrics into an oblong measuring 16-1/2" x 59". Cut the ends at an angle as shown.

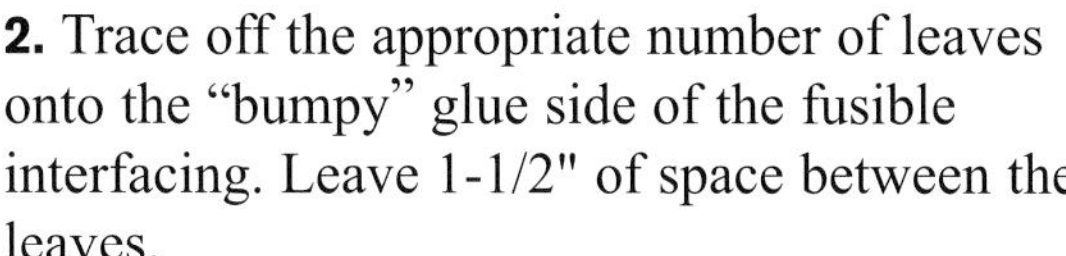

2. Trace off the appropriate number of leaves onto the "bumpy" glue side of the fusible interfacing. Leave 1-1/2" of space between the leaves.

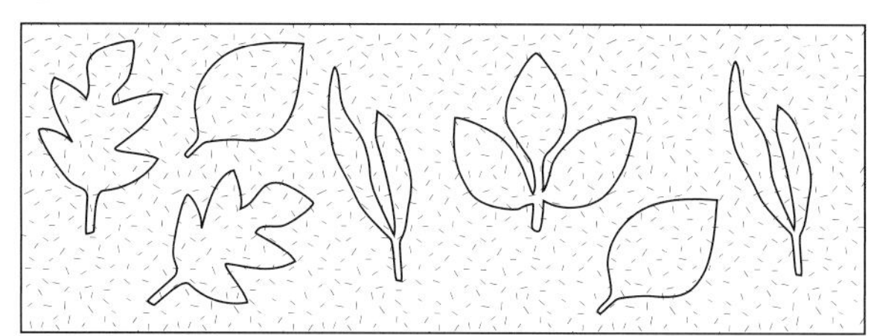

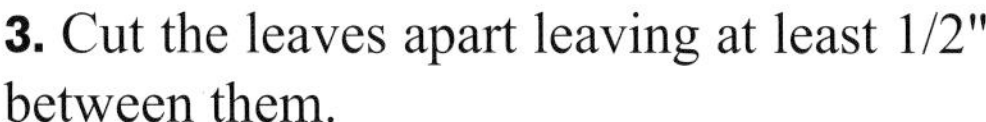

3. Cut the leaves apart leaving at least 1/2" between them.

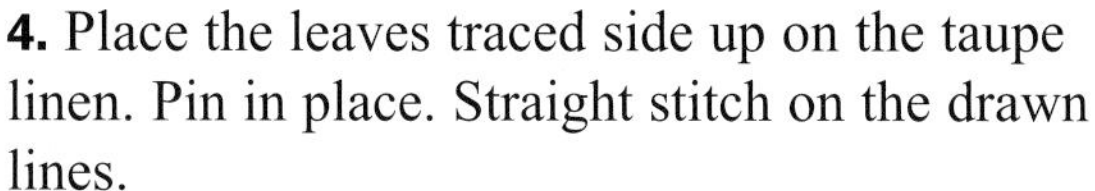

4. Place the leaves traced side up on the taupe linen. Pin in place. Straight stitch on the drawn lines.

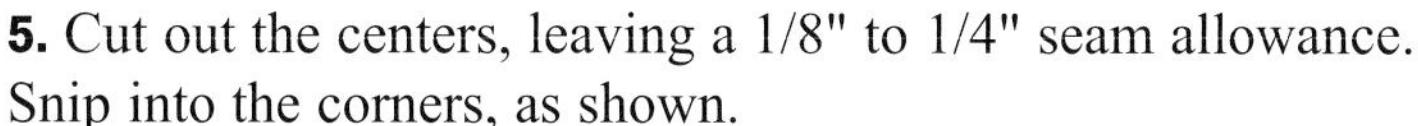

5. Cut out the centers, leaving a 1/8" to 1/4" seam allowance. Snip into the corners, as shown.

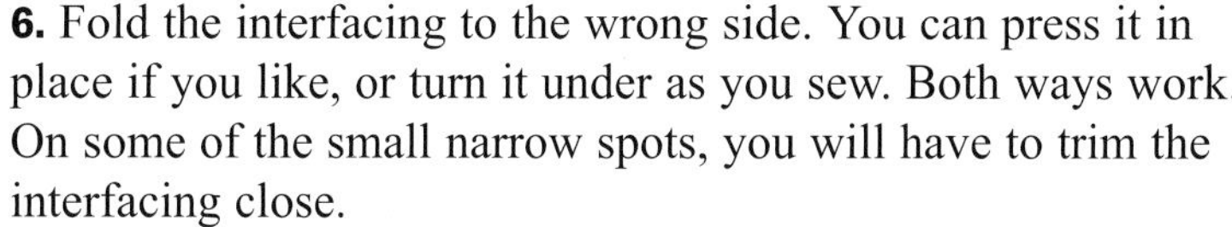

6. Fold the interfacing to the wrong side. You can press it in place if you like, or turn it under as you sew. Both ways work. On some of the small narrow spots, you will have to trim the interfacing close.

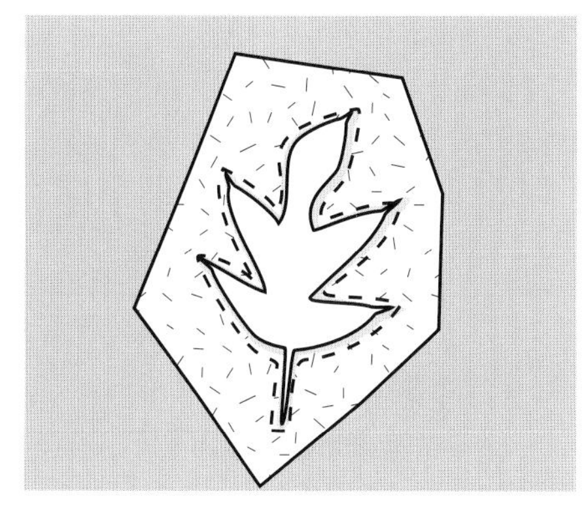

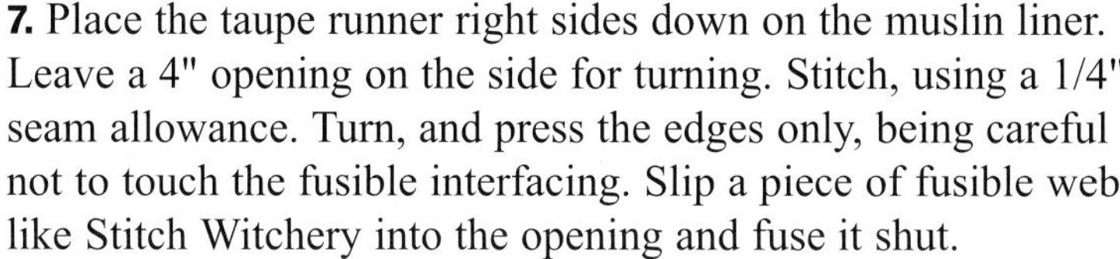

7. Place the taupe runner right sides down on the muslin liner. Leave a 4" opening on the side for turning. Stitch, using a 1/4" seam allowance. Turn, and press the edges only, being careful not to touch the fusible interfacing. Slip a piece of fusible web like Stitch Witchery into the opening and fuse it shut.

8. Lay the runner flat and pin around each leaf.

9. Stitch on the taupe linen, using a small zig zag, 2 width and 2 length. An open-toe appliqué foot enables you to see better. An alternative is to place the runner in an embroidery hoop or use a darning foot and stitch free motion. See pages 89-91 for directions.

10. Stitch the veining details with a regular straight stitch or a straight stretch stitch.

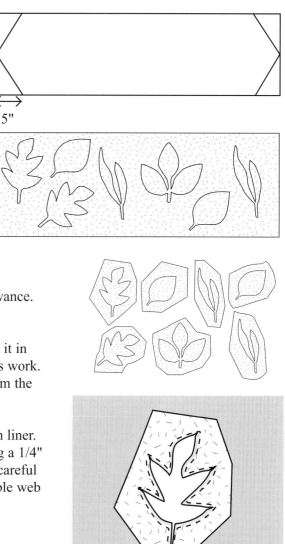

Candlewicking is a hand technique that has been used for decorative purposes for hundreds of years. America is the country candlewick embroidery originated in, and it is one of the few needle arts to start here. Originally it was mainly used to decorate bedspreads. Candlewicking evolved for two reasons—it is basic human nature to have pieces of beauty or significance surrounding us. During the late 18th century, fine fabrics and yarns were scarce and expensive in America. Cotton fabric and embroidery thread were accessible and economical, so the American women embellished their bedspreads with these materials.

Candlewicking uses a heavy cotton thread or cord and is mainly French knots and chain stitching, although any traditional embroidery stitch is useable in candlewicking. Traditionally, candlewicking is a combined tone on tone pattern or design. In the original period for candlewicking, the base fabric was a firm twill weave cotton that had been bleached in the sun. Usually candlewicking is stitched on muslin in tone on tone colors.

For our machine candlewicking techniques, we chose to make a bell pull and a baby's sleeping pillow.

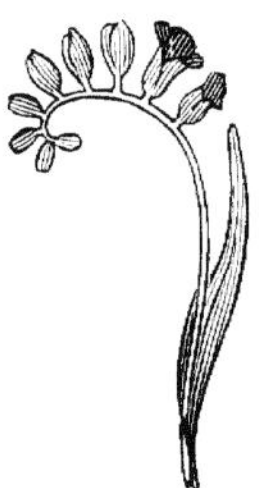

Bell Pull

This would be pretty hanging in a long narrow area, or as a part of a wall arrangement. Bell pulls may be any size needed to fit the space.

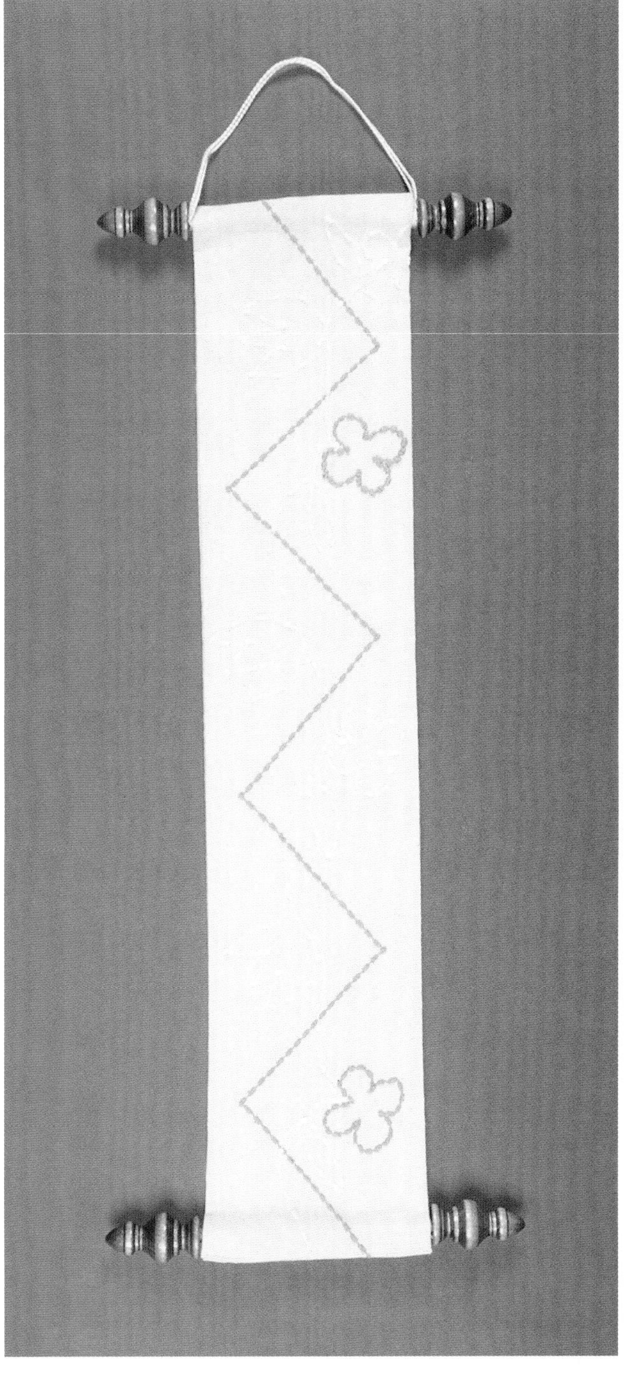

Materials needed:

2 pieces of muslin, 5" x 20-1/2"
Stabilizer (we used an adhesive)
Buttonhole or jeanstitch thread; we used tan and white
Cotton or polyester bobbin thread
Size 100, 110, or 120 sewing machine needle
Bell pull ends (wood or metal). Can be purchased at a craft or needlework shop.
12" cord or ribbon for hanger
Water soluble marker
Machine foot with a tunnel to allow the "knots" to feed under the foot. {A candlewick foot if available, a piping/cording foot (that is not straight stitch), a bulky overlock foot, or even an embroidery foot}.

Computer machine settings:

Program into memory:

(a)zig zag stitch set at 2 width, 0 length, enter this seven times into memory; (b) straight stitch width 0, length 2, enter 2 times. The setting of the stitch length in (b) determines how far apart the French knots will be. Change this length to meet the needs of the project.

Manual machines:

Set machine for (a) above, complete this then set it for (b) and switch back and forth as you progress through pattern.

1. On right side of one muslin piece, draw or trace the pattern with water soluble marker.

2. Set machine as above.

Pattern shown 50% of actual size

3. Attach presser foot, as described above. Have feed dogs in up position.

4. Insert large size needle.

5. Thread with regular bobbin thread in bobbin, jeanstitch, buttonhole twist or topstitch thread in needle. You may want to loosen the upper tension slightly.

6. Begin stitching and guide fabric so stitching stays on marked lines. When the "knots" are being made, there will be little forward progress.

7. We sewed the tan lines first, both the zig zag and then the flowers. For this we used a shorter stitch length on the (b) machine setting.

8. Change to white heavy thread, set machine at the longer straight stitch length for (b) machine setting.

9. Follow pattern; we tried to sew in a continuous line as much as possible.

10. We found it easier to let the end thread tails be loose, and then pull them to the wrong side when the area was complete. To do this, a fine crochet hook or a snag-nab-it tool could be used. A seam sealant can be applied to wrong side where the threads were pulled through to prevent them from fraying.

11. Rinse finished piece to remove any pen marks that still show and let dry.

Assembling pull:

1. Press candlewicked piece on wrong side, use a velvet board or thick terry towel under the candlewicked piece. (This allows the knots to sink into the depth and not be flattened.)

2. With right sides together, sew side seams of the bell pull. We used 1/2" seams, but you might want to double check the dimensions of your pulls prior to sewing. Stop sewing l-1/4" from either end and anchor stitching. Fold unsewn parts even with sewn edges.

3. Sew top end (5" side), catching folded ends to hold them in.

4. Turn piece so right side is out, and press seams. On unsewn edges, press them in also.

5. Fold open ends in, and topstitch close to edge of pull.

6. Insert bell pull holders. On the wooden ones we used, the ends came loose and could be pushed back on.

7. Tie hanger cord onto pull top. Press if need be, and enjoy!

Quick Project

"Shhh" pillow

Sometimes when baby is sleeping, it is nice to have a warning sign out to deter siblings, grandparents, cousins or whomever to stay out so baby gets its beauty sleep. Our little pillow is a subtle reminder. If you like, it could also be candlewicked on the opposite side with a bold AWAKE, but usually awake is pretty obvious!

1. Trace design onto right side of one muslin piece. Lay other one aside for now.

2. Set machine as above.

3. Begin stitching letters, and continue until all are candlewicked.

4. Pull thread ends to wrong side as above.

5. Rinse marker out. Press dried piece as explained.

Materials needed:

2 pieces muslin 6" x 5-1/2"
20 inches pre-gathered 1/2" wide lace
White jeanstitch/buttonhole thread
Large size needle as above
Small quantity fiberfill
11" cord to use as hanger
Water soluble pen

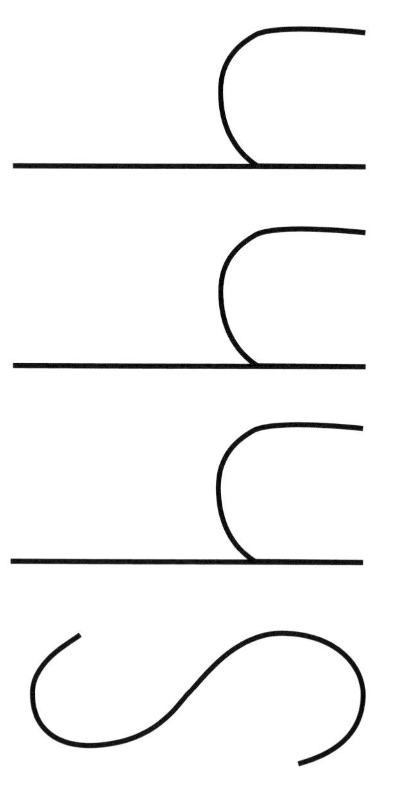

Assembling pillow.

1. Attach hanging cord to top of pillow 1" from pillow ends.

2. Apply lace to right side, by lining up gathered edge of lace on the 1/4" sewing line, and basting it in place. At ends, be certain to fold at a 45 degree angle so raw edges will not show. Also make a tuck in each corner.

3. Place back, right sides together over front and lace.

4. Starting at lower edge, stitch back to front. Leave a two inch opening at bottom. Turn, right sides out.

5. Stuff with fiberfill.

6. Press.

7. Fold seam lines to inside. Stitch opening shut with a narrow top stitch.

8. Hang on doorknob to alert people that baby is getting the needed rest.

Look in the oldest photos or paintings you can find and you will see the couching technique used. Soldiers, royalty and common people used this technique to embellish their uniforms or special attire. Of course, in those days, it was hand stitched and very costly to have sewn. It is currently very popular on ready-to-wear clothing, and in home decor. It is a very simple technique to sew.

Couching is simply sewing over threads or cords that are too heavy to be put through the eye of a needle. It is also a good way to combine several threads to get your own "personal" effect. When couching, you can use an invisible thread to hold the cords in place or use a decorative thread for a totally different effect. If you are sewing a narrow thread, or several threads combined, it is best to use a zig zag stitch wide enough to cover the threads and hold them in place. If you are using a wider cord to pipe (such as the middy braid), a straight stitch works fine.

Free Motion Embroidery

Free motion embroidery can be traced back to the first treadle sewing machines. While they revolutionized the world by enabling the family's clothing to be sewn in a fraction of the time it took by hand, the more adventurous embroiderers were quick to see the potential for embroidery as well! Old books show magnificent examples of intricate embroidery, all done on a straight stitch treadle sewing machine.

Free motion, as the name implies, gives you the freedom to stitch freely in any direction. You are not limited to forward and back, but can sew sideways, diagonally or in circles. Sometimes we use a zig zag and sometimes a straight stitch fits the bill. This is a technique that requires some skill on your part, and a little practice goes a long way. We always emphasize this to our students—not to discourage them, but to make sure they understand that if their first efforts aren't to their liking, better results will follow with a bit of experience under their belt.

Any machine can be used to do free motion embroidery. The set up list must be followed closely, and includes solutions to possible problems as well as information on how to set up your machine for free motion embroidery. Before you begin, be sure you clean your machine and if your machine requires oiling, it should be oiled. A smooth running machine in good operating condition is a must.

Set up list:

1. Remove the presser foot and, if necessary, the shank or ankle it attaches to.

2. Put in a new size 80 universal needle.

3. Drop or cover your feed dogs. If you don't know how to do this, look in your instruction manual under "How to sew on a button." It will tell you there. If your machine does not have the capability to drop the feed dogs or cover them, which a small number of machines don't, put your stitch length to "0." They will only go up and down, not try to move the fabric forward.

4. Set the machine for a regular straight stitch. If you have dropped the feed dogs, the stitch length doesn't matter. If you can't, or have a cover that fits over them, set your stitch length to "0."

5. Place your fabric in a hoop by placing the larger part of the hoop on a flat surface, lay the fabric on top of it, and insert the smaller hoop inside.

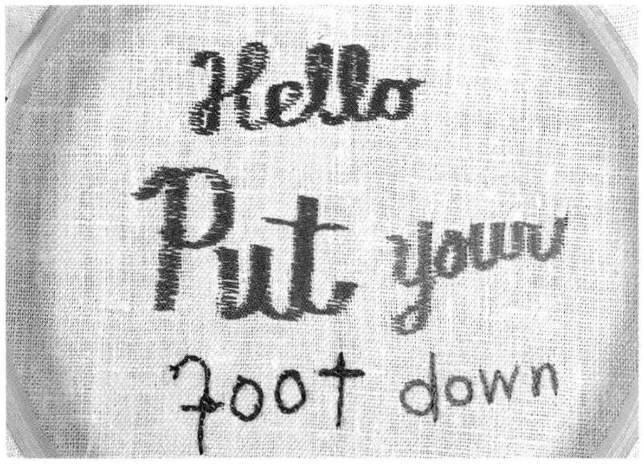

"Hello" is stitched with a 4 width zig zag, and regular sewing thread; "put" is stitched with a 5 width zig zag and quilting thread; "your" is stitched with a 3 width zig zag and topstitching thread; "foot" is stitched with a straight stitch and topstitching thread; "down" is stitched with a straight stitch and quilting thread.

Random straight stitching with regular thread.

Straight stitching with regular thread, experimenting with different fill techniques.

6. Thread your machine with the presser foot lever in the up position. This opens the tension disks and enables the thread to drop down between them. For practice, begin with any good quality regular sewing thread.

7. Place a bobbin, wound with 60 wt. (fine), in the machine. This thinner than usual thread will not build up bulk and will enable you to stitch with all different weights of thread on top and not have to change bobbin to match the top thread. White is the usual choice, but the fine threads are also available in colors or black.

8. Insert the hoop with the fabric in the sewing machine and lower the presser foot lever. Lowering the presser foot lever engages the tension. That means it squeezes the disks together, putting tension on the upper thread. If you forget to do this (and YOU WILL!), you will get "wads" of thread underneath, sometimes referred to as "thread throw-up." Because it is on the underside of the fabric, many embroiderers start to adjust the bobbin tension. That's not the problem. The problem is that the top thread isn't being held in tow by the tension disks, so it gets out of control and goes everywhere and in essence, the bobbin wins the "tug of war." We often suggest to our students that their first free motion embroidery project should be a sign that reads, "PUT YOUR FOOT DOWN!"

9. Start sewing slowly and moving the fabric randomly. You are moving the fabric! If you don't move, it won't go anywhere. You will move the hoop in the direction you want to go; don't rotate the hoop. Try doing some loops and circles. Try writing your name.

10. Draw some simple shapes, circles, squares, triangles on your fabric and stitch on the drawn lines. This will give you practice following shapes. Try to fill them in different ways, squiggles, solid lines, crosshatch, or try going over the same line many times as we did in the zig zag line.

11. Now set your machine to zig zag and repeat the above exercises. Start with a 4 width. Move sideways, diagonal, up and down. You are creating the stitch length by the way you move the hoop. If the stitches are too spaced out, move the hoop slower and run the machine faster. Try some at a 3 width, a 2 width, and try writing your name.

12. Draw some simple shapes, triangles, ovals, circles and some lines. Experiment with different widths, directions, and types of fills.

13. Now let's experiment with different weights of thread. When using topstitching, remember to use a size 100 universal needle, or a topstitching needle. We used a 4 width zig zag.

14. Switch to a straight stitch and play some more. Notice that the fine weight of thread is very delicate and almost disappears.

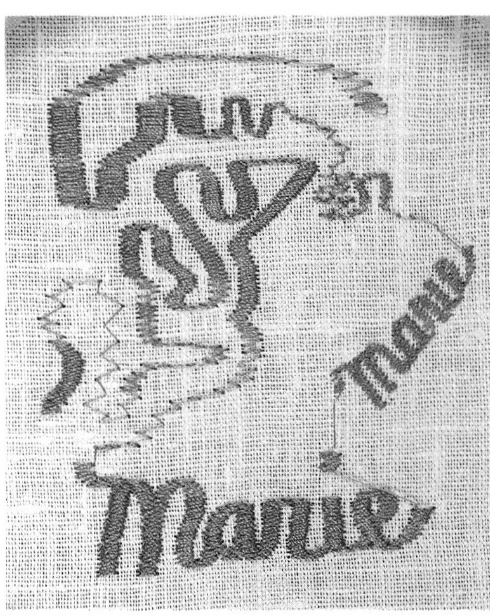

Zig zag sampler with widths varying from 2 to 5 using regular sewing thread.

You have now graduated from Free Motion 101! Pick a project and move on.

Zig zag widths varying from 2 to 5, using regular sewing thread and practicing following lines.

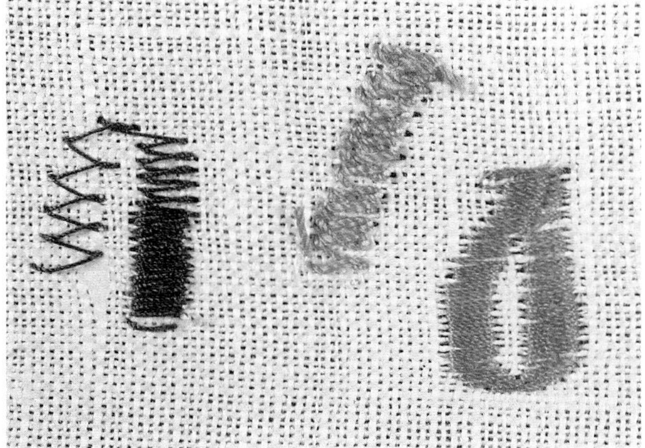

The pink is quilting thread, the orange is topstitching thread and the turquoise is fine embroidery thread. The width for all is 4.

The lavender is topstitching thread, the green is quilting thread and the turquoise is fine embroidery thread. A straight stitch was used for all.

Crewel Embroidery

Crewel embroidery, also known as Jacobean embroidery, is characterized by its gloriously rich colors and unique designs. Eastern influence, enthusiastically embraced by the English embroiders, and coupled with the Tudor tradition of delicate floral and tree motifs, produced a unique look and feel that we know today as Crewel embroidery or Jacobean embroidery.

Many designs incorporate a tree or tree branch combining florals, fruits, leaves and unique variations quite unlike any that grow here on earth! Intertwined are often found the birds, beasts, butterflies and other members of nature, traditionally worked in wools, with soft shades of greens, blues, and browns, intermixed with the reds, yellows, purples and other brighter colors of nature.

Photo Album

For our crewel embroidery, we created our own design; if you have access to traditional crewel designs, go for it! Or you can use a combination of traditional with your own variations. We used remnants of crewel yarn from a project we had at least started years ago. Some of them did come to completion! If you do not have leftovers to use, buy a very light weight, such as DMC Floralia, and separate the strands. We used a method of sewing called bobbin work to create our crewel design. The decorative yarn was put in the bobbin case and an invisible thread was used in the top portion of the machine.

Materials needed:

Extra bobbin case (if available, or otherwise loosen tension screw on bobbin to allow yarn to flow easily). *ALWAYS REMEMBER: IF YOU LOOSEN THE REGULAR BOBBIN CASE, SCREW TO TIGHTEN IT THE SAME AMOUNT WHEN YOU RESUME REGULAR SEWING!*
Fine yarn - we used 3 shades of green, two shades of dark brown, rust, and yellow.
Invisible thread for upper machine thread
Marking pencil
Spring needle, or darning presser foot
Muslin: one 15" x 32" piece, two 10-1/2" x 13" pieces
Two 8-1/2" x 11" pieces of cardboard (we used the backing from tablets)
Glue gun and glue sticks
(1) photo album; ours was 11" x 11-1/2" x 3"

1. Place the 15" x 32" muslin around your album. Mark the area where you want your design. Trace pattern with marking pencil or pen onto WRONG side of fabric. Be sure to think through so design ends up on the front, and right side up.

2. Fill bobbins. You can do it by machine and hold the yarn in your hand, or hand wind the bobbin yourself. Remember the yarn is thicker than thread, so does not hold as much yardage. We found it best to wind two or three bobbins with a color, then they just needed replacing when they ran out in the center of a design.

3. Place filled bobbin in case and into machine. Bring up the bobbin thread/yarn.

4. Remove presser foot or put on darning foot. If using spring needle, put it in position now.

5. LOWER presser foot lever.

6. You will be sewing on the wrong side of fabric and yarn will be on right side, but you can not see it as you are stitching! We want to acquire a relatively long stitch as that allows the yarn to have texture and depth. You are moving the fabric. Where you set the stitch length doesn't matter.

7. Drop or lower the feed teeth.

Our Illustrations are shown in color, for clarity, even though you won't be able to see the colors as you sew.

8. Start by filling in stem of flower. Use one of the shades of green. We worked with a straight stitch and moved to follow shape of stem. Do not fill in complete stem—that is where the shading comes in. Continue with a different shade of green.

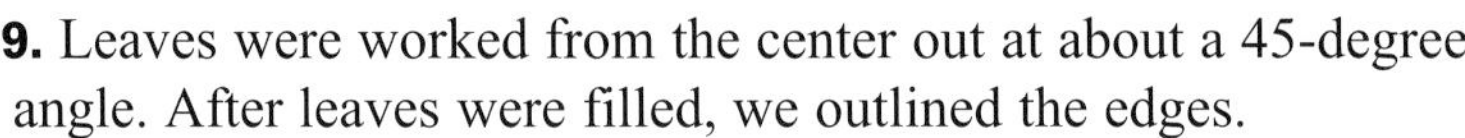

9. Leaves were worked from the center out at about a 45-degree angle. After leaves were filled, we outlined the edges.

10. We marked off sections of the flower where we wanted color changes just to give an idea. It does not matter if one is a little less and one a little more. We started with one of the dark brown shades for the flower and worked a straight stitch shaping the lines to conform with the edge of the petal.

(We found it easier to pull the ends of yarn to the wrong side as we came to the end of a color or section. Use a snag-nab-it tool or a fine crochet hook.)

11. Next we switched to the other dark brown shade and continued filling to cover the fabric.

12. The rust was stitched next to fill in the center portion. HINT: You can see the stitching on the top side, even though you cannot see the colors you are working. If you peek, you will be able to gauge how close you have to stitch to fill in the flower.

13. The yellow highlights were the next step, and then the circular center.
14. Press on wrong side on velvet board or thick towel to allow the yarns to maintain their depth.

Assemble:
1. Heat glue gun.

2. Lightly measure fold lines and even them out.

3. Place photo book in centered position, being certain decorated portion is right side up and on front.

4. With glue gun, apply glue to inside cover (one side at a time, as it dries fast). We found it easiest to glue the top and bottom sections first. Fold fabric onto glued portion. Slip fabric under binder ring bar for a neater effect. Stretch fabric as you are gluing it to be taut. Repeat with front inside cover. Then glue and fold fabric into back. Be certain book cover will close, but be taut.

5. Allow glue to dry.

6. Glue small pieces of muslin over cardboard.

7. Glue covered muslin over raw edges of fabric on front and back covers of album.

There—you have just made a unique gift. These are a good gift for special occasions. For a special wedding anniversary or similar event, one of these special albums provides a place to put the pictures of the event, as well as special notes and cards.

Quick Project

Felt Needle Case

This is a handy case for storing your hand or sewing machine needles when traveling. The inner insert stores them well and protects them. If you wish, you could paste a small pad of paper in here and use it as a card tally instead.

Materials needed:

Two 7" x 4" pieces white felt
One 4" x 2-1/2" piece of white felt
Light weight yarn: cranberry, pink, yellow and dark green
Marking pen
Darning foot or spring needle
Black latch bobbin case (as explained above)
Monofilament thread

1. Trace design to wrong side of one of the 7" x 4" pieces of felt.

2. Insert filled bobbin.

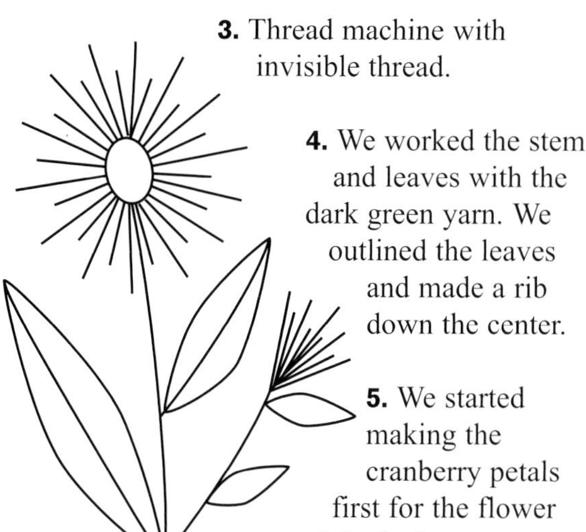

3. Thread machine with invisible thread.

4. We worked the stem and leaves with the dark green yarn. We outlined the leaves and made a rib down the center.

5. We started making the cranberry petals first for the flower and the bud.

6. Next we worked the pink lines.

7. The centers were filled in with the yellow in a circular motion.
8. Pull yarn ends to wrong side.

To assemble:
1. Fold 2-1/2" x 4" piece in half , bringing the 2-1/2" sides together.

2. Stitch to center portion of undecorated piece of felt. We used a decorative stitch and regular sewing thread. (Feed dogs raised for this).

3. With a fabric glue, glue the two felt pieces together.

4. Trim with pinking shears if desired and allow to dry.

Brazilian Embroidery

Brazilian Embroidery is characterized by its three-dimensional flowers, textured threads and bright colors. The leaves and flowers jump out at you in all their glory, placed on a delicate intertwining background of graceful field flowers and beautiful foliage! It shines with shiny threads, metallics, beads and hot, bright colors.

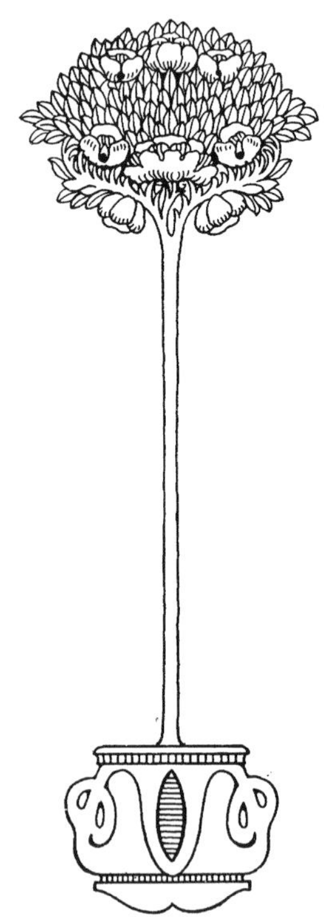

We are offering you alternatives, depending on your skill level, the variety of threads available to you and the type of design you choose. We will break down our embroidery into two parts: First, the base design; and second, the three-dimensional flowers and leaves.

As with any skill worth doing, practice is necessary to perfect the moves and techniques. Begin by practicing basic free motion set up and stitching as described on pages 89-91. Then choose a design and try out the different threads and techniques that follow. When you feel confident, start on your project. It is necessary to work with the fabrics or a similar fabric and the threads you intend to use. We found the thread that looked great on muslin was lost on our boiled wool fabric. More on that later; let's get on with Brazilian Embroidery by machine!

Materials needed:

Assorted threads: to thread through the machine needle, try machine quilting thread, rayon embroidery thread, topstitching thread, various heavier weights of cotton embroidery thread. To couch over, try pearl rayon, hand crochet thread, DMC rayon floss, Mokuba's boucle or any shiny cords or yarns.

Thread to match the couching threads or invisible thread.

Assorted fabrics, muslin, lightweight linen or broadcloth, heavier weight, denim, boiled wool or Polarfleece

5" to 6" machine embroidery hoop

Sewing machine with straight stitch and the ability to drop or cover the feed dogs

Serger tweezers

"Snag-it" tool (a miniature latch hook sold to repair snags in sweaters) or a crochet hook

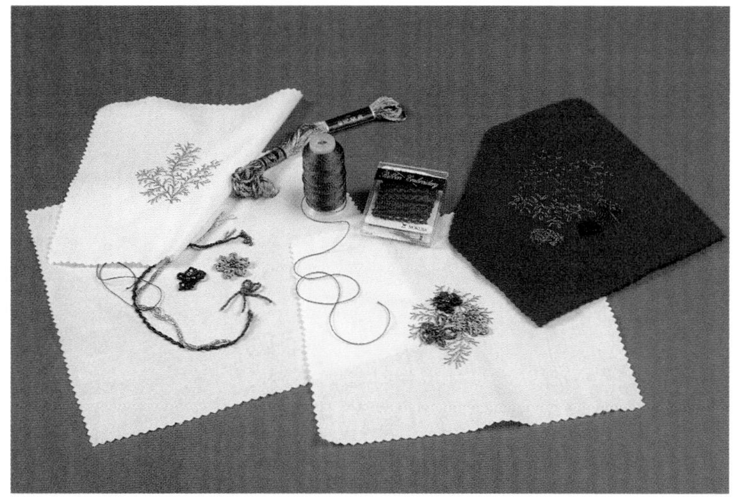

1. Set your machine up for free motion machine embroidery according to the directions on pages 89-91. Thread your machine with heavier weight sewing thread like quilting thread, topstitching thread or 30 wt. machine embroidery thread. Set the machine for straight stitch. If desired, trace off one of the base designs onto your fabric or just jump in and start stitching! Either way, sew slowly; you may want to set your sewing speed to slow if you have that option on your machine and continue sewing until you have a nice base design. Notice how the first base design has a bottom, and the other radiates out from the center. Try going over each section twice. Try laying a piece of pearl rayon couching thread on the fabric and couching over it as you go for a heavier effect on fuzzier fabrics such as boiled wool or polar fleece.

2. Now we will do some twisted cord flowers. Choose some couching weight threads, boucles, pearl rayon or rayon floss. Set your machine for straight stitch, basic free motion embroidery set up. Thread the needle with regular weight thread to match your couching thread, or with invisible thread. Anchor the end of the thread by taking a few stitches across it. A serger tweezers is very helpful to hold the couching thread in place.

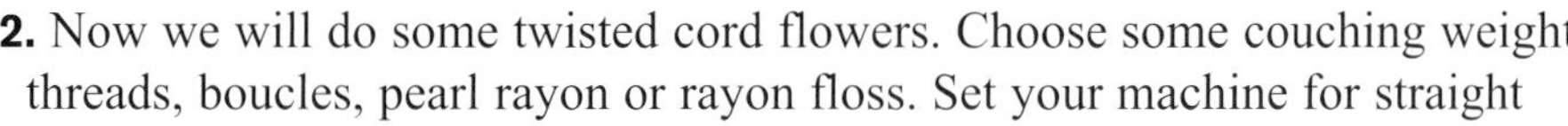

3. Using the "snag-it" or a crochet hook, hold a loop of thread to the right, and anchor the end to form a loop as shown.

4. Twist the snag-it tool to twist the thread until it "kinks."

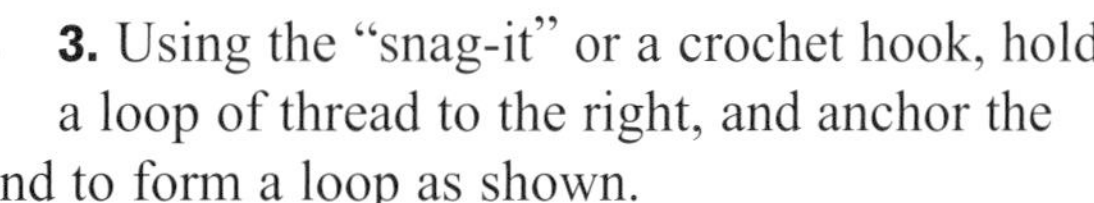

5. Grabbing the twist in the middle with the serger tweezers, bring the "snag-it" tool to the sewing machine needle. Let go with the tweezers and the thread will twist back on itself. Anchor the end the "snag-it" tool is holding with a couple stitches. You have a great twist to anchor and make a flower with. Just bring the finished end in to form a loop and stitch in place.

6. Continue the above steps until you have 5 to 7 loops. Add some beads to the center.

7. These are the techniques we used on our boiled wool hat and mittens, along with a French knot. The French knots are really easy. Anchor a bumpy type thread such as a boucle at the end of the thread.

8. Wrap it around the needle loosely, and take a stitch to anchor it.

9. Continue to wrap and anchor several more times and cut the cord. There is your French knot!

Now let's make our boiled wool hat and mittens. "Boil up some wool" by finding <u>100% wool</u> sweaters and alternately washing and drying them in the washing machine. If possible, use a hot water wash/cold water rinse setting. When they have "felted," another term for shrunk, they are ready. We had several sweaters with moth holes, so we recycled them into a whole other life! An alternative would be polar fleece.

Materials needed:

3" and 5" embroidery hoops
Raspberry and burgundy boiled wool or polar fleece
Commercial pattern for hat and mittens
Couching threads: dark green pearl rayon, burgundy boucle for French knots, mauve and plum rayon floss
Regular sewing thread to match couching threads or invisible thread, dark green quilting thread or 30 wt. machine embroidery thread
"Berry" color beads for flower centers

1. Begin by stitching the base as we did in our practice session. Carefully place your 5" hoop in the center of the hat where you want the design to be and simply fill the hoop with the base design. We found we had to couch a strand of pearl rayon along with our green free hand stitching to achieve the results we wanted.

2. Add flowers with beaded centers and French knots surrounding them.

3. Using the smaller hoop, repeat a smaller version on your mittens.

4. Lastly, construct the hat and mittens according to pattern instructions.

Quick Project

Christmas Ornament

For our Christmas ornament, we used some leftover scraps of linen, assorted threads from our hat and mittens, boucle cord to edge it, and a luxurious tassel to finish it off.

Materials needed:

5" embroidery hoop
(2) 6" squares of white linen or linen like fabric
Couching threads: green pearl rayon, green boucle, burgundy boucle, mauve rayon floss
Regular sewing thread: white, and colors to match couching threads, green quilting thread or 30 wt. machine embroidery thread for base design
"Berry" color beads
Burgundy tassel
A "handful" of fiberfill

1. Using an air soluble marker, trace off a 3" circle in the center of one linen square. Use a glass, small hoop or whatever you have on hand that is approximately 3" across.

2. Using green quilting thread, follow the above directions and stitch a base, filling the circle.

3. In the center, using the mauve rayon floss, make an extra long twisted cord. Make a French knot with it. This forms a rose. Let it build up a bit in the center, for dimension.

4. Continuing with the burgundy boucle, make additional French knots into roses.

5. Using a matching regular green thread on top, or invisible thread, make twisted cords with the green pearl rayon at the base of the roses. We used green boucle around the center rose and pearl rayon around the remaining roses and buds.

6. Finish by threading up with invisible thread or regular green thread and sewing beads randomly among the base.

7. Complete your ornament by placing the embroidery right sides together with the other linen square. Thread your machine with regular white sewing thread and stitch 1/4" from the edge of the circle, leaving a 2" hole to turn. Cut close to the edge with pinking shears and turn.

8. Press and stuff lightly with fiberfill. Carefully zig zag the hole shut, maintaining the circular shape.

9. Thread with invisible or matching thread. Make a long twisted cord with the burgundy boucle and couch it around the ornament. Form a hanging loop at the top with a length of boucle and tack it in place. Tack on the tassel at the bottom and enjoy.

Blackwork

Blackwork, sometimes known as Spanish work, is a monochrome embroidery, worked with high contrast between the embroidery color and the background fabric. Typical Blackwork is stitched in black thread upon a white fabric. Such embroidery has Moorish origins and was first mentioned in England in Chaucer's Canterbury Tales, written at the beginning of the 16th century. The main use of Blackwork in England until the beginning of the 18th century was decorations for household items and clothing. Blackwork remains essentially an embroidered art form. The dramatic contrast of black on white and the geometric shape of the designs fascinate embroiderers and non-embroiderers alike.

For our Blackwork projects, we went contemporary with a desk set, and everyone's (or almost everyone's) favorite theme—golf. This would be a good gift for man or lady, either all three pieces or a portion of them. Any theme is adaptable to black work; as you will see, it can be a scene, object, or lettering.

Betty has a set of hand-done Blackwork pictures hanging in the dining room that have been there a long time. They always receive compliments from new visitors to the room. Your machine-done Blackwork articles will draw compliments also.

Materials needed:

Even-weave fabric: (these sizes can be adjusted to size of objects you have)
9-1/2" x 6-1/2" for pencil holder
11" x 24" for 7" x 9-1/2" date book
24" x 13" for 18" x 12" calendar/desk pad
DMC black cotton size 50 machine embroidery thread
White or ivory bobbin thread
Desk pad, date book, can for pencil holder (we used a 12-ounce orange juice can)
Water soluble marker
Open toe embroidery presser foot

Desk Set

Monthly Planner
Monday
Tuesday
Wednesday
Thursday
Friday
Saturday
GOLF

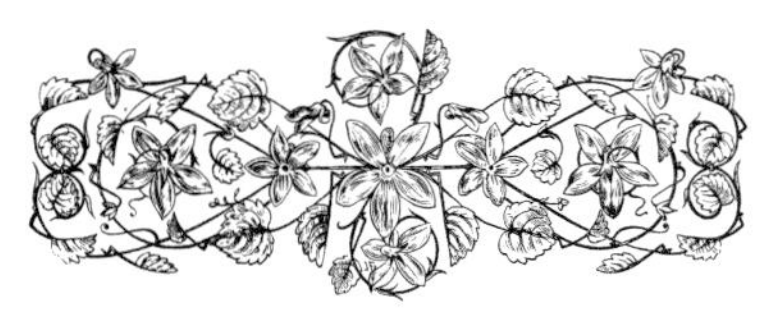

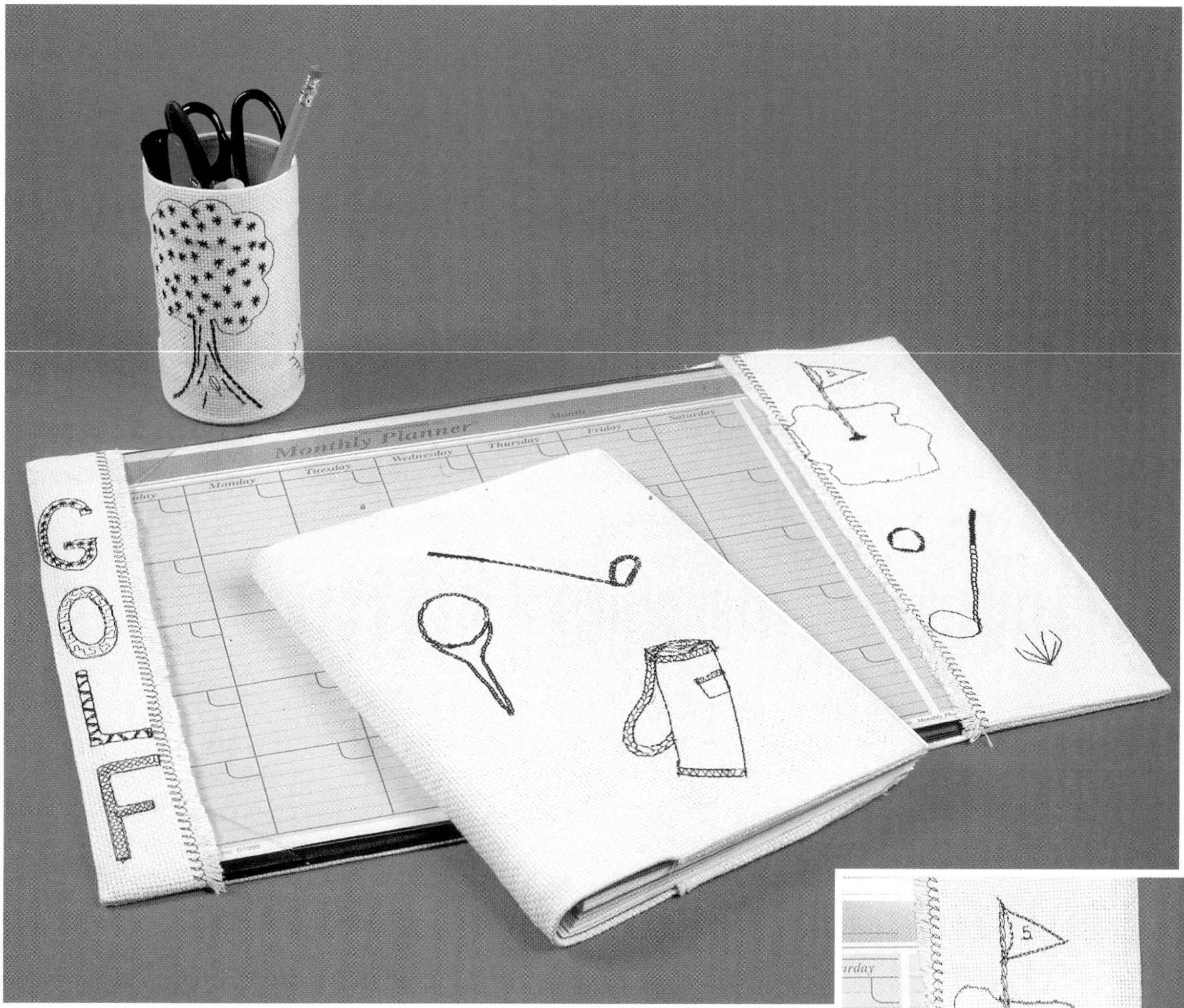

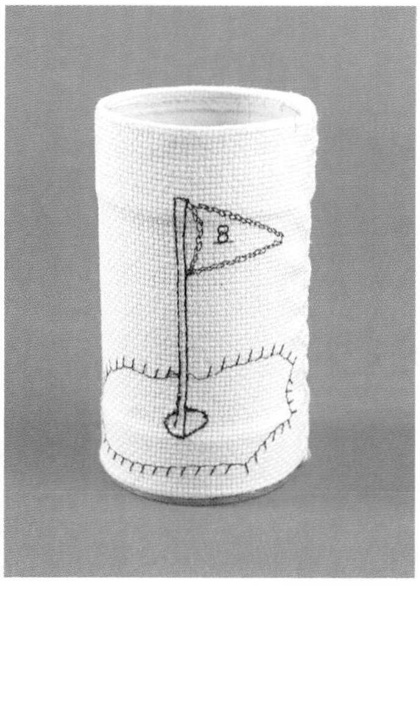

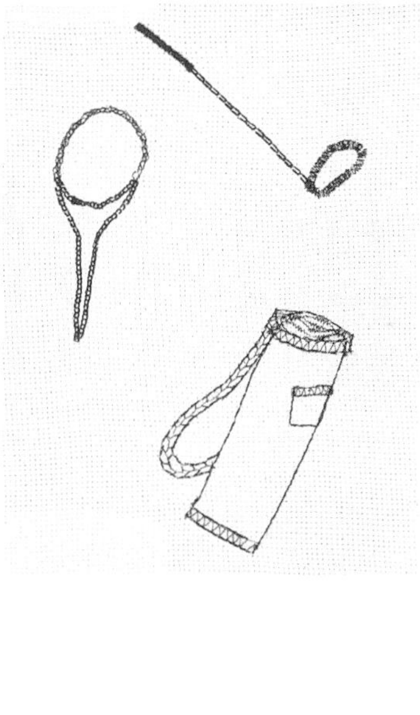

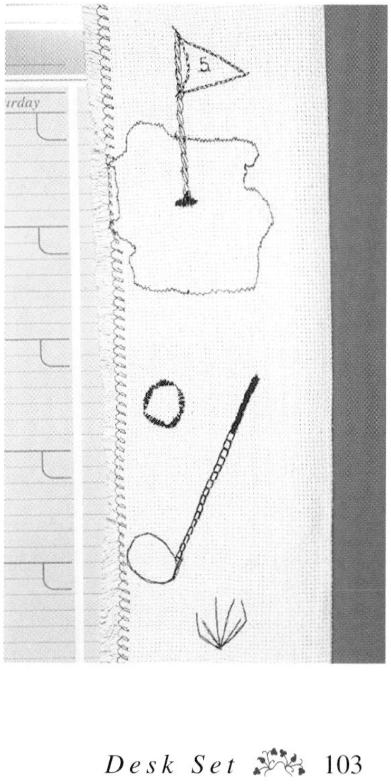

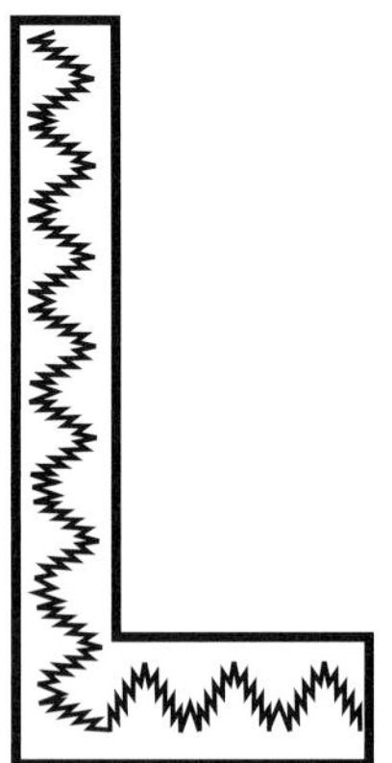

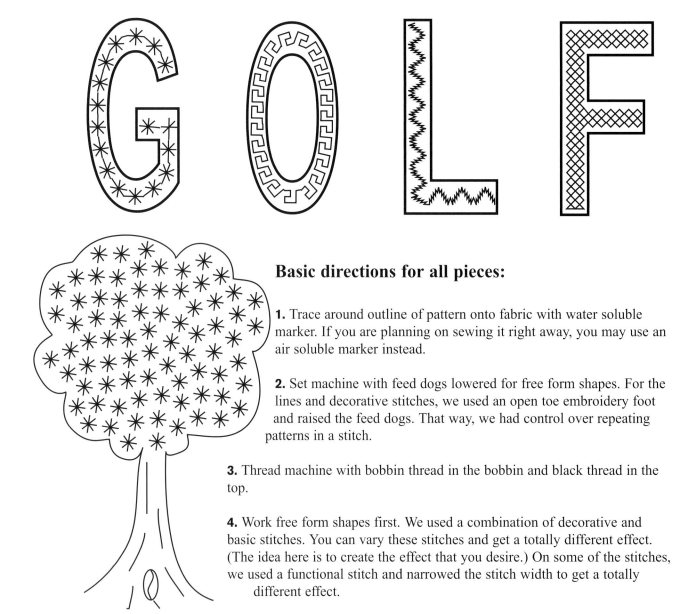

Basic directions for all pieces:

1. Trace around outline of pattern onto fabric with water soluble marker. If you are planning on sewing it right away, you may use an air soluble marker instead.

2. Set machine with feed dogs lowered for free form shapes. For the lines and decorative stitches, we used an open toe embroidery foot and raised the feed dogs. That way, we had control over repeating patterns in a stitch.

3. Thread machine with bobbin thread in the bobbin and black thread in the top.

4. Work free form shapes first. We used a combination of decorative and basic stitches. You can vary these stitches and get a totally different effect. (The idea here is to create the effect that you desire.) On some of the stitches, we used a functional stitch and narrowed the stitch width to get a totally different effect.

5. Work straight lines and decorative stitches with the feed dogs raised, so the finished effect looks pleasing.

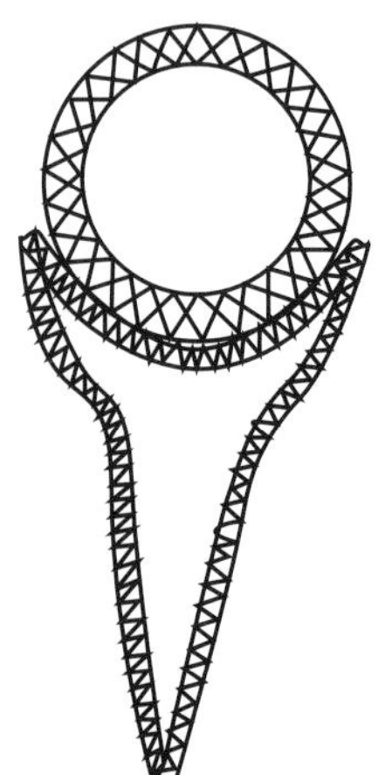

Assembling the pieces:

Pencil holder:

1. Fold long ends of finished piece to wrong size (measuring so they just cover the cylinder). Press.

2. Press under raw edges on one short end.

3. Wrap finished cover around cylinder. Be certain folded under edge is on the outside when overlapping two ends. Hand stitch this with an invisible stitch, so it is held on tightly. Voila. It is completed!

Date book:

1. Measure cover and fold under long ends on long sides of book cover. Press.

2. Measure cover and fold under flaps, so that cover is taut, but book will lay flat when closed. Press.

3. Fold these ends right side together.

4. Stitch to end of inside flap, trim seams if needed.

5. Where inside flap ends, sew the folded under part to just meet where the flap ends. Our seam was about 1/8" from edge.

6. Turn and press.

7. Place flaps over covers of date book.

Desk mat:

1. Finish short ends with a decorative stitch. We placed our decorative stitch about 1/2" from edge and then fringed up to it.

2. Repeat steps 2 through 7.

When you have your completed set on your desk or it has been given as a gift, enjoy the compliments.

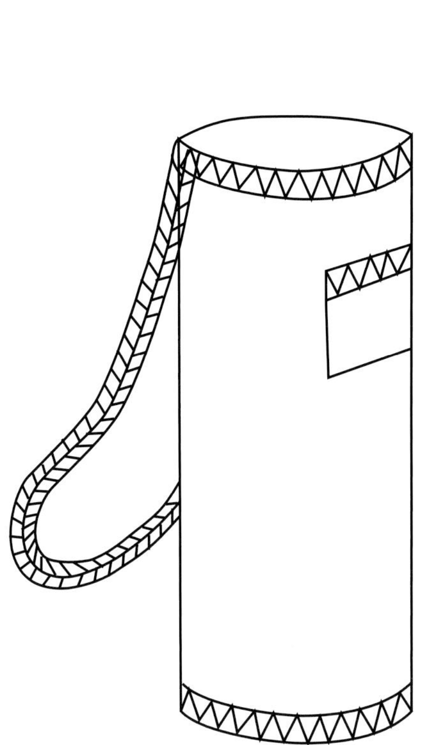

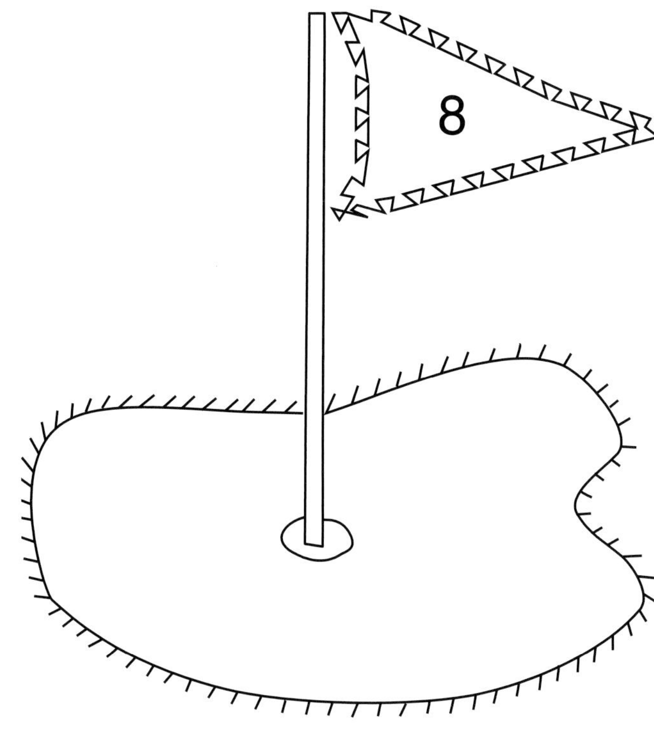

Quick Project

Felt seems like a good base fabric to use; it will not scratch the glasses, it holds its shape and is fairly sturdy. Glass cases have a way of getting misplaced, so extras of these are always useful. Make several and you will be prepared for quick gifts when needed. Any pattern could be used. We chose to give a visual picture of the use of the stored item.

Materials needed:

2 pieces of felt 9" x 7"
DMC black cotton embroidery thread
Adhesive stabilizer
Open toe presser foot

1. Place adhesive stabilizer on wrong side of one piece of felt. Lay other piece aside for now.

2. Set up machine with open toe presser foot and thread as above.

3. Using an air or water soluble marker, trace the "eye" design on the right side of the felt.

4. Have feed dogs raised to satin stitch outside of eye.

5. Lower feed dogs and stitch eyelashes in curves.

6. Set machine with an overcast stitch, but work with feed dogs lowered to make it easier to turn curves for circle.

7. The words were made using letters available on the sewing machine. They could be stitched free hand.

8. Remove excess adhesive stabilizer from stitched portion of case.

9. Place second piece of felt next to wrong side of embroidered piece.

10. Stitch two pieces together along upper edge using any decorative stitch.

11. Fold in half, short ends together.

12. Round the lower corner on the unfolded side.

13. Stitch all layers together on two sides using a decorative stitch.

14. If edges of felt have shifted during stitching, trim them to even. Apply seam sealant to thread ends to prevent raveling.

Enjoy, and keep your glasses from getting scratched.

Stumpwork
(Padded Embroidery)

Stumpwork, or padded embroidery, is three-dimensional in effect. It has a raised surface, consisting of stuffing, molds of wax or wood, or simply bunched threads, forming the base for the figure, which is then covered in fabric or thread and then decorated. Everything was used: bits and pieces of fabrics and trims, beads, lace and even human hair have been found. These figures are then applied to a background fabric and embellished around.

The name may have come from "on the stamp," as a stamped background was usually used to place the figures on. From the end of the 14th century, ecclesiastical vestments were sometimes decorated with metal threads laid over thick linen threads, then couched. During the 1600s, panels with religious themes were often made into pictures, mirror frames or boxes. Stumpwork projects illustrated the life and times of the embroiderer. The hairstyles, clothing, and surrounding motifs provide insight into the life, manner, dress and customs of the ladies creating the embroidery.

Today, padded work is enjoying a revival amongst embroiderers and quilters alike. It incorporates many techniques, embroidery, beading, appliqué, "Blackwork" embroidery and many more. We've created a design for you, encompassing many of the old subjects, typical flower motifs, a rabbit, straight out of the 1600s, the usual profusion of bugs, and, of course, a snail; but we replaced the ladies and gents from that era with a delightful pair of children sure to win your heart!

Because of the variety of skill levels, machinery available, and wide choice of possible materials, we are giving you lots of alternative choices in both technique as well as materials. Experiment and above all, have fun! When you are ready to graduate and design your own stumpwork designs, coloring books have great motifs that would be very suitable. In the essence of stumpwork, anything goes! Every nook and cranny is filled and proportion and perspective are unknown. We got great inspiration and feel for stumpwork from a variety of books from the library. We've listed them in the bibliography.

Stumpwork Wall Hanging

Although the traditional books on the subject of Stumpwork mention it being worked on satin, we chose linen, as we thought it would hold up better for our purposes without snagging. The background fabric could be satin, linen, or any number of other woven white fabrics. We don't go into a detailed materials list because we are using bits and pieces of so many things. This is a project to experiment with what you have on hand and substitute where needed. We will also give you alternate techniques so if you aren't comfortable with free motion embroidery, you can substitute appliqué. Or if you have a new machine with embroidery capabilities, you can use that instead of free motion embroidery.

Materials needed:

1/2 yard white linen or other woven fabric for background
Assorted scraps of fabric, lace, trims, and ribbon for children's clothes
Assorted Ultrasuede and/or felt scraps (used because they don't fray)
3/8 yard un-bleached muslin for children and "lawn"
3" x 10" blue felt for pond
Assorted beads, black and other colors
Assorted colors of threads: hand/machine quilting, topstitching, rayon or cotton embroidery, metallic and regular sewing thread
White 60 wt. cotton for the bobbin
Air soluble marker, water soluble marker, Sulky iron on transfer pen, or dressmaker's carbon paper
1/8 yard for inner frame(we used gold calico)
1/2 yard for outer frame and back (we used houndstooth check)
1/2 yard fleece
Handful of fiberfill
Universal sewing machine needles #80 and #100
Sewing machine with some decorative stitches
Painted dowel for hanging

1. Trace off the master pattern onto paper and transfer it onto your linen, leaving an extra fabric border of 3" on each side for hooping. If you can see through your fabric, you can transfer it by tracing it using a wash-out marker. An alternative is to trace the master pattern on your paper using the iron on transfer pen and then iron it on to your fabric. A third alternative is to use dressmaker's carbon paper to transfer the design. Choose the best alternative for your fabric, keeping in mind that you may not cover all the markings; and the ability to remove any marks showing when you are done is important.

2. Trace off the "children" onto the un-bleached muslin, being sure to leave sufficient fabric around them to hoop. We will create our "children" then cut them out, stuff them and sew them down to the background fabric. We need to "build" our figures from the back forward. Start by stitching their faces. They are very simple, just a smile, using a straight stitch and small circles for eyes. The smile could be done free motion, see pages 89-91 for details, or use the straight stretch stitch instead. (An alternative would be a permanent fabric marker). For the eyes, we embroidered small circles free motion. You could use beads or a black permanent fabric marker.

3. Let's dress them. Forget "ladies first," we started with our little gentleman. A scrap of houndstooth suiting was lying on the table and jumped up and said, "I'd make great shorts!" So that's what we did. This is a woven fabric, so we cut a rough shape, larger by 1/4" than the drawing, and stitched it down using invisible thread. This can be done free motion or with a standard zig zag, 2 width and 2 length. Poke the edges under as you go.

HINT: A stiletto, a long, blunt instrument with a handle used to hold things in place instead of your fingers, is invaluable for this kind of sewing.

4. Red Ultrasuede was a perfect choice for his jacket. Felt is a great alternative. Because they don't fray, we didn't need to worry about turning the edges under. We stitched it in place with invisible thread and added the black outlines down the front and on the sleeves with quilting thread. Stitch several times free motion or use the straight stretch stitch. Red Ultrasuede shoes applied with invisible thread complete the outfit. Because his hands are on top of his jacket, they need to be applied last. We had some beige Ultrasuede so we used that, but you could use felt or your original muslin, but with the muslin you need to cut it larger and turn under the edges. Use invisible thread. The last touch was his beaded buttons. Because it gets in the way, we will apply the hair after we attach our young gentleman to the background.

5. On to our young lady. Stitch or draw her face as for the little boy. We had a scrap of red plaid flannel we used for her dress, but it could be almost anything. Cut and apply as for the little boy's shorts; 4" of leftover lace became her collar and apron. Attach with invisible thread. Black Ultrasuede shoes complete her ensemble. Apply hands as in step 4.

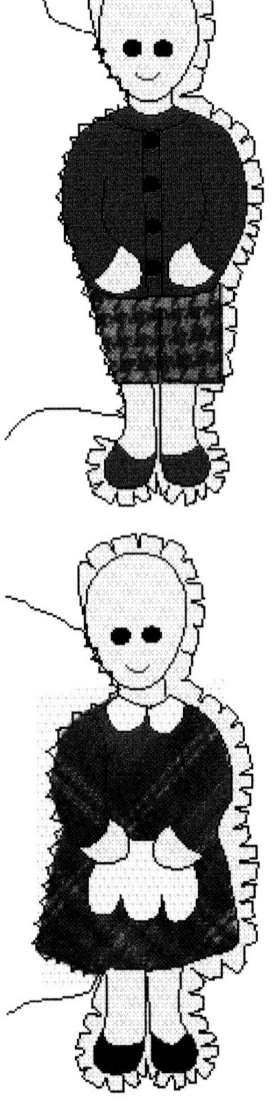

6. Now we're ready to stuff them and apply them to the background fabric "on the stamp," as they say. Cut them out, leaving 1/4" extra all the way around. Clip into the curves and points. Place them in position on the background fabric. Tuck under the edge as you go and stitch one side.

7. Without removing it from the machine, poke a little fiberfill under the figure. Don't stuff very much, as it will distort the background fabric.

8. Now attach some hair, using a heavy thread like top stitching thread or bits of lightweight yarn. Stitch it in place in the middle using invisible thread. We tied mini bows and tacked them on each side of our little girl's pigtails.

9. On to the tree. The trunk is stitched with a heavy th like topstitching thread or pearl rayon. We used a chai stitch. This can be done with the foot on or free motion. It's done the same way in either case. Thread your sewing machine with invisible thread. Cut off 18" or so of the chaining thread and tack it in the center.

10. Stitch forward 3 stitches and stop with the needle down in the fabric. Cross the chaining thread in front of the needle. Stitch 3 stitches and repeat.

11. Our leaves were stitched with a built-in decorative stitch. You may or may not have this exact stitch, but many machines do have it or a similar one. Experiment on a scrap to get a similar look. If you don't have a similar stitch, try tapering the width on the zig zag as you sew, starting at 0 width at the tip of the leaf, widening it to 4 or 5 and tapering it back to 0. The length remains the same, at about 1/2. Use your open toe appliqué foot to help you see better. Another alternative would be to cut out leaves from Ultrasuede or felt and stitch them on.

12. Our house is Ultrasuede, stitched down with a blanket stitch outline. We used quilting thread to give a heavier handstitched look. The windows and doors are Ultrasuede, straight stitched in place, again with quilting thread. A bead completes the doorknob. The roof is a wide row of oversewn satin stitching. Stitch the satin stitch with your widest width, 1/2 length zig zag, then go back down the center with a straight stretch stitch. It sort of "bunches the threads," creating a pleasant design. The chimney is Ultrasuede with straight stitched bricks, sewn with quilting thread.

13. Reminiscent of Blackwork embroidery, the hilly lawn was created separately and then attached "on the stamp." Cut the general shape from unbleached muslin, leaving an extra 1/4" to tuck under. Choose a decorative stitch and sew rows, next to one another to cover the area. We stitched it down using a small blanket stitch and about half way around, we stopped and tucked a puff of fiberfill in to pad it a bit.

14. The bush, on the right-hand corner of the house, is stitched free motion, using topstitching thread. This is the heaviest thread that can be placed in the needle of your sewing machine. Use a size 100 universal needle because it has a large hole. Use fine cotton in the bobbin. Place your fabric in a hoop and following the directions for free motion stitching on page 89-91, set your machine for straight stitch and create a long and short stitch. The same threads and stitches were used on the flower, just below the house and lawn. The flowers to the left of the house were created the same way but with quilting thread, which isn't quite as heavy.

15. Our cloud was stitched separately and attached. We used a fine silver thread and did miniature stippling, meandering free motion stitching. Then we cut out the cloud and stitched it to the background fabric with invisible thread. The sun is Ultrasuede, stitched on with gold quilting thread in a combination of the blanket stitch and straight stitch highlights.

16. The fish pond is worked the same as the cloud, using a green metallic thread on blue felt. After it was applied to the background with invisible thread, we stitched a scallop border around the edge of the pond with one of our decorative stitches. The fish has a beaded eye and is made from Ultrasuede. The lily pad is stitched with couched green yarn and a bit of silk ribbon looped and tacked down on top with a yellow beaded center. The couching can be done free motion or with the foot on. Use invisible thread. Coil the yarn in place, and hold with a dab of glue stick. Then stitch.

17. The grass at the children's feet, the bunny, and the flowers to the right of the children are all done free motion, using the straight stitch and quilting thread. See pages 89-91 for details. The beaded stems above the bunny and below the lawn are straight stitched free motion with quilting thread, and beads are tacked on the tips of the branches as you go.

18. All that's left are the creepy crawlies. They're so cute. The caterpillar at the base of the tree is individual scallop stitches, stitched side by side, with straight stitch legs and beaded eyes. The snail, next to the bunny, is free motion with quilting thread and beaded eyes. The lady bugs, bumble bee and beetle are made from Ultrasuede, glued in place and embellished with beads and free motion straight stitched details. The butterfly has free-floating wings. They are made from Ultrasuede, embellished with decorative stitches, and tacked on to the body which was stitched free motion with quilting thread and a beaded eye.

19. To finish your wall hanging, place your embroidered panel on a double layer of fleece. Measure and mark around your design, leaving about 1/2" on each side, and coming to the bottom of the pond and the top of the cloud. Cut four strips of the inner fabric 1-1/2" wide and 4" longer than each edge. Press under 1/4" on one long edge of each strip. Lay the strips in place and line them up with your lines. Fold the ends under, creating mitered corners. Pin, press, and sew the mitered corners. Lay it back on your embroidery and check the fit. Pin through all the layers and attach with a blanket stitch. Repeat with the outer layer. We stitched with invisible thread this time, as a contrast thread would have gotten lost on our houndstooth checks.

20. Trim any excess fleece or linen and cut a backing piece the same size as your front. Cut four hanging tabs 3" x 5". Fold in half right sides together, lengthwise, and stitch using a 1/4" seam allowance. Turn and press. Fold in half, matching the raw edges, and place the tabs evenly spaced across the top of the hanging, starting 1" in from each edge. Pin in place. Place the embroidered panel right sides together with your backing piece and sew, using a 1/4" seam allowance. Leave a 3" hole to turn. Trim the corners and turn right sides out. Press and hand stitch the hole shut. Insert a dowel for hanging and enjoy.

Quick Project

Ladybug

Business Card Case

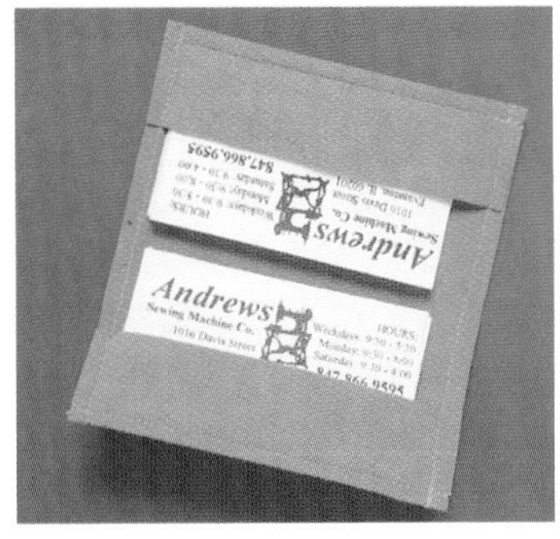

1. Choose your favorite bug to practice on and put it on a business card case. Cut 1 piece of Ultrasuede 4-1/2" x 7-1/2". Following the diagram for placement, create your favorite bug following the previous instructions. Fold on the marked lines and stitch near the edges.

1-1/4"
Fold
2-1/2"
Fold
2-1/2"
Fold
1-1/4"
4-1/2"

Hardanger Embroidery

Hardanger Embroidery, the more common form of drawn thread work, originated in a mountainous district in Norway. The people of Hardanger are famed all over the world for this beautiful openwork embroidery. Characterized by little rectangular groups of satin stitches known as "kloster" blocks, arranged to outline the cut spaces, they build up the major portion of the design. Hardanger embroidery is suitable for linens, bedspreads, tablecloths and napkins, and is often found in church needlework on altar cloths, chalice veils etc. A linen, linen type fabric or aida cloth is needed. These fabrics are referred to as evenweave, as the threads are the same spacing in both directions.

We have adapted Hardanger to the sewing machine by utilizing a heavier than usual thread, top stitching thread, in the needle, and leaving a regular weight sewing thread in the bobbin. Our "kloster block" is sewn with a basic zig zag. We duplicated other designs with simple decorative stitches. All are based on the satin stitch, which is the zig zag, or a variation of it, at a short length and wide width. We graphed out designs for linen guest towels, and as our quick project, some designs for Christmas ornaments or coasters. We will be giving you specific information on tension, stitch length, etc., but remember to try it on a scrap of the fabric you are using and experiment yourself with the different threads and settings.

We offer you some designs with cut-out spaces and some without. The sewn item will be more durable in the wash without cut-out areas. Our finished towels measure 13" x 17", but that could certainly vary according to your needs.

Linen Guest Towels

Materials needed:

1 yard white 100% linen 58"-60" wide
2 spools white topstitching thread
Regular white sewing thread
Sewing machine with zig zag and optional decorative stitches
Small sharp trimming scissors
Schmetz size 100 universal sewing machine needle

1. Cut your linen into 6 pieces, 14" x 18". Pull a thread to indicate the cutting line to be sure you cut on the grain.

2. Press a 1" hem at the bottom of the towel, folding it toward the right side. The stitching we will be doing must be done from the right side, and by pressing the hem to the right side, we can see the raw edge to cover it accurately. You may want to machine baste the hem in place at this point.

3. Set your machine for a zig zag stitch. Try a 4 width and a 1 length. Thread the top of the machine with topstitching thread, and regular thread in the bobbin. Use the #100 universal needle. Experiment on a scrap to get the right tension, so the top thread pulls just slightly to the back. We found the tension needs to be set to a lower number than normal. Because our linen was stable, we found we didn't need a stabilizer on the back. If you are getting puckering, try a tearaway stabilizer on the back. See pages 9-10 for stabilizer information.

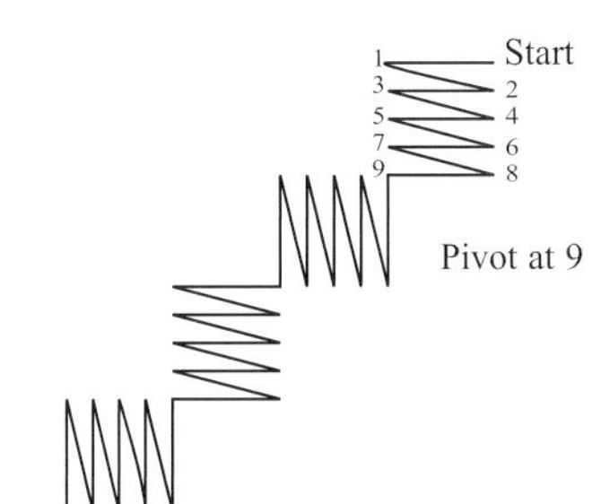

4. Now you are ready to sew your hem in place. Use the zig zag stitch to create a satin stitch, covering the raw edge of the linen as you sew.

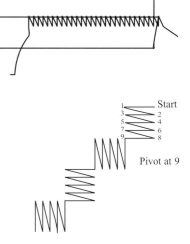

5. Let's practice our klosters on a scrap. We want to achieve approximately a square. Using a 6 width zig zag, at a 1 length, we got a pleasing result. You want your threads to lay one next to another; if they are bunching up or too spaced out, adjust the length of your stitch. The width will be dependent on your sewing machine. You probably want to use 6 if you have it, otherwise the widest you have. A kloster is a group of stitches forming a square. With our settings, 9 stitches created a square. Your results may vary, depending on your stitch width and length settings. Try stitching 9 stitches, then pivoting a quarter turn. Stitch another 9, etc.

6. To change direction, you need to stitch a 10th stitch and then pivot.

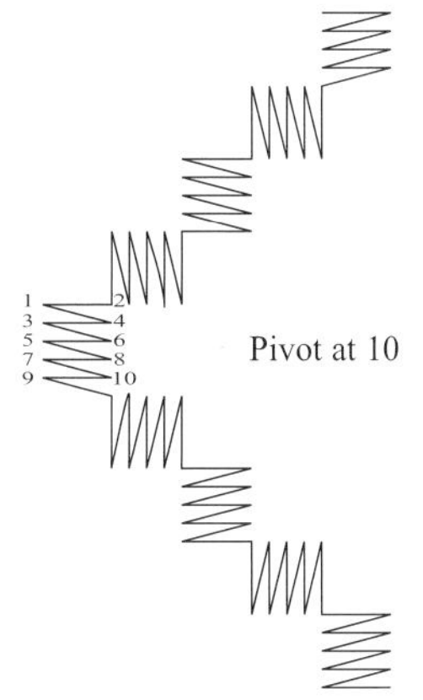

7. This is the basis for the "zig zag" design on our first towel. After you are satisfied with your sample, begin about 3" above your hem and stitch a row all the way across the towel. Begin your second row one "kloster's" distance below your first. The second row should just connect at the corners, as shown.

8. Complete a third row and then cut out the areas indicated. Use a sharp, small trimming scissors. The cut areas can be reinforced with a Fray Check type product.

9. Our remaining towels use a combination of decorative satin stitches. These are decorative stitches built in to your machine, or on older machines available on cams or seam formers. Experiment on scraps to determine the best machine settings. Then do rows, combining the different possibilities. When possible, connect them to form an enclosed area that can be cut out.

10. When done, square up the towels and hem the remaining three sides.

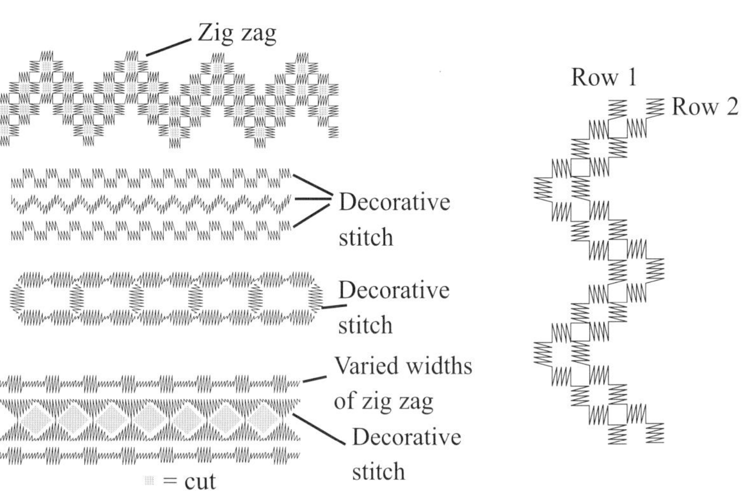

Quick Project

Ornaments/coasters

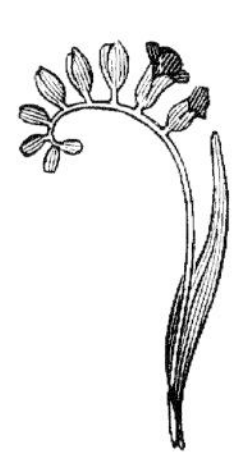

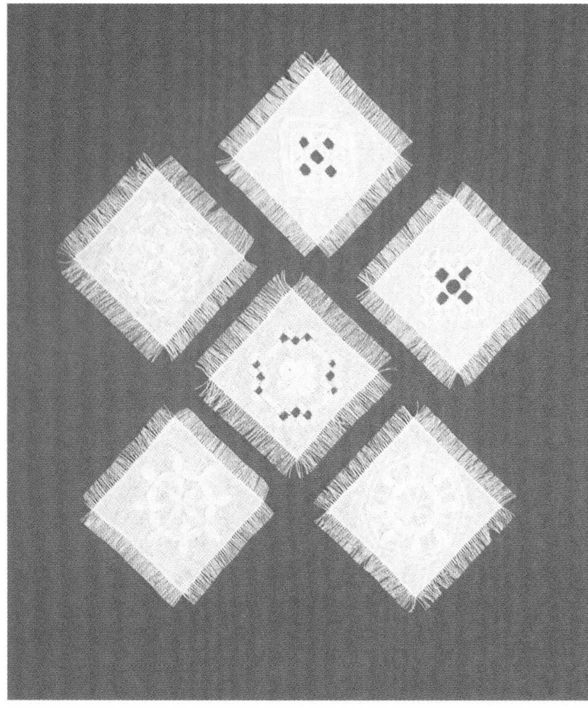

Our quick project can be used either as a Christmas tree ornament or as coasters. They are designs, round or square, about 3" to 4", stitched on Aida cloth and fringed. They are a fun way to try out your stitches and settings.

Materials needed:

1 pkg. 22 count Aida Cloth, white (sold for counted cross stitch)
1 spool white topstitching thread
Regular white thread for the bobbin
Sewing machine with zig zag and optional decorative stitches

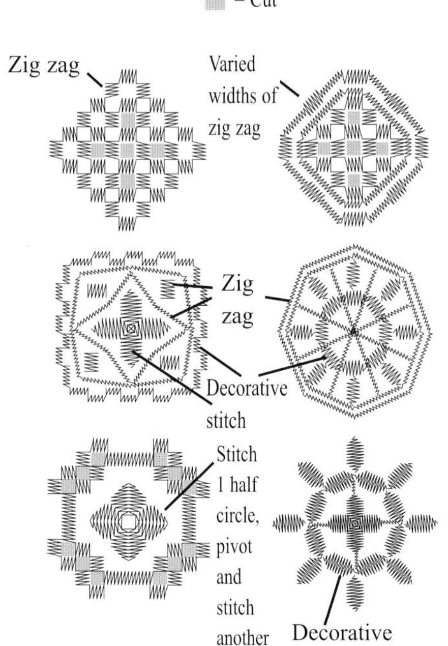

1. Our first ornament is constructed with "klosters." See page 117 for basic directions. Stitch from the center out.
2. Our others are variations of the "klosters" combined with decorative stitches. See the illustration for details, and don't be afraid to experiment with your own designs and stitches.

3. When done, measure and mark an equal distance on each side, about 1/2", and pull a thread to indicate the edge. Zig zag on that line, using a 2 width and 2 length.

4. Cut 1/2" out from your line of zig zag stitching, and fringe the edge. For ornaments, attach a hanging string to a corner.

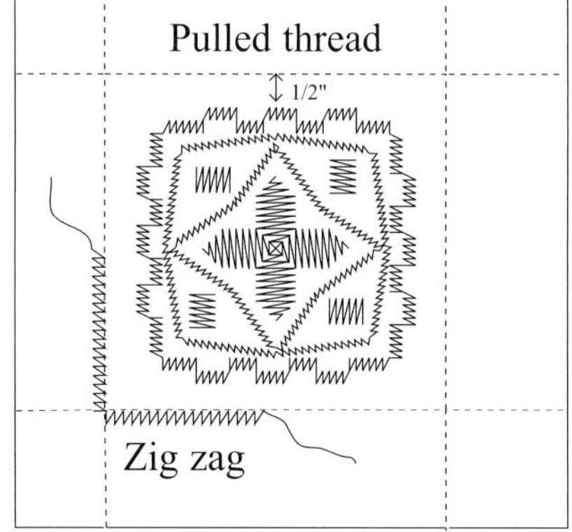

Swiss Embroidered Trims

The beauty of the Swiss embroidered trims has been admired through the centuries.

We chose a traditional little girl's dress as our project for the embroidered trims. While we finished our edges with a scallop stitch, these trims are also magnificent when combined with other laces and trims purchased or made by you. While we chose colors for our embroidery, a white-on-white or color-on-color embroidery can be stunning and very rich looking. The rayon embroidery threads give a very nice shimmer to the design, but a cotton embroidery thread can be equally elegant. Do use good quality embroidery threads for this project.

Materials needed:

Child's dress pattern with collar
Colored cotton batiste as called for in the pattern
1/2 yard white batiste or cotton organdy for creating the embroidered trim
Assorted machine embroidery threads; we used green, pink, purple, peach, blue, yellow and white
60 wt. cotton bobbin thread
Regular sewing thread to match colored cotton batiste
"Stitch & Ditch" paper stabilizer or a similar stabilizer that will not leave a residue showing
Sewing machine with decorative stitches

1. Cut out the dress from colored cotton batiste following the instructions, but set aside the collar pattern piece for now.

2. Measure the bottom circumference of the dress. This is the length we need to make our strip of trim. Measure the bodice length, adding a little extra, to give you the amount of trim you need for the bodice strips. Add these two measurements together, plus an extra 6". Using this measurement as the length and 4" as the width, cut strips of white batiste or organdy. Seam them end to end to create one long strip. You want to try to create all the embroidery at once, as it entails changing thread colors. So, we will stitch all the green first, then the blue, etc. As we continue, keep in mind you will probably not have the exact stitches we used, but you will have something similar.

3. Thread your machine with 60 wt. fine cotton in the bobbin and green embroidery thread on top. Place two layers of "Stitch & Ditch" stabilizer under the fabric. Choose a leafy vine type stitch, similar to ours. Practice on a scrap until you find the right tension setting. The upper tension needs to be lowered until the bobbin thread does not show on top. Use your appliqué foot, (see page 13). Stitch the leafy vine the full length of your white batiste strip.

4. Look at your stitching and decide where a point about 1" to 2" apart is a good spot to stitch your first flower. We will repeat that flower the full length of our leafy vine. To do this, thread your machine with blue thread, and choose a flower stitch. If you have a "single pattern option," engage this now. This is a feature on computerized machines that allows you to stitch one of the patterns, and then stop

automatically. If you don't have this option, stitch on a scrap until you are at the beginning of the stitch. Then carefully watch and stop at the end of the flower. Stitch one flower and stop. Lift the presser foot and without cutting the threads, move to the next spot and stitch the next flower. Continue until all the blue flowers are done.

5. Place your yellow thread on top and choose a different flower. Stitch all the yellow flowers, as we did the blue flowers.

6. Because we love purple, we did purple flowers on both sides of the stem.

7. A liberal dose of pink is always good.

8. Peach got only one flower.

9. To stitch the collar, begin by tracing it off on your white organdy or batiste fabric, marking the sewing line as well as the cutting line with an air soluble marker. Stitch a single motif, as shown, for each side of the collar. Be sure to put stabilizer underneath. Tear off the stabilizer when you are done.

10. Place your collar pieces, wrong sides together, on another piece of organdy or batiste, large enough for both collar pieces. Thread your machine with white embroidery thread and choose a scallop stitch for the edge; stitch it around the collar on the stitching line, going through all the layers. Place your stabilizer underneath the stitching lines.

11. Stitch on either side of the strips of embroidery, about 1/2" from the edge of the flowers. Our finished strip ended up to be 1-3/4", but yours may be wider or narrower. Place stabilizer underneath the strips.

12. Now find a good TV show and snip the threads, tear off the paper and trim your scallops.

13. Finish the dress according to the pattern directions.

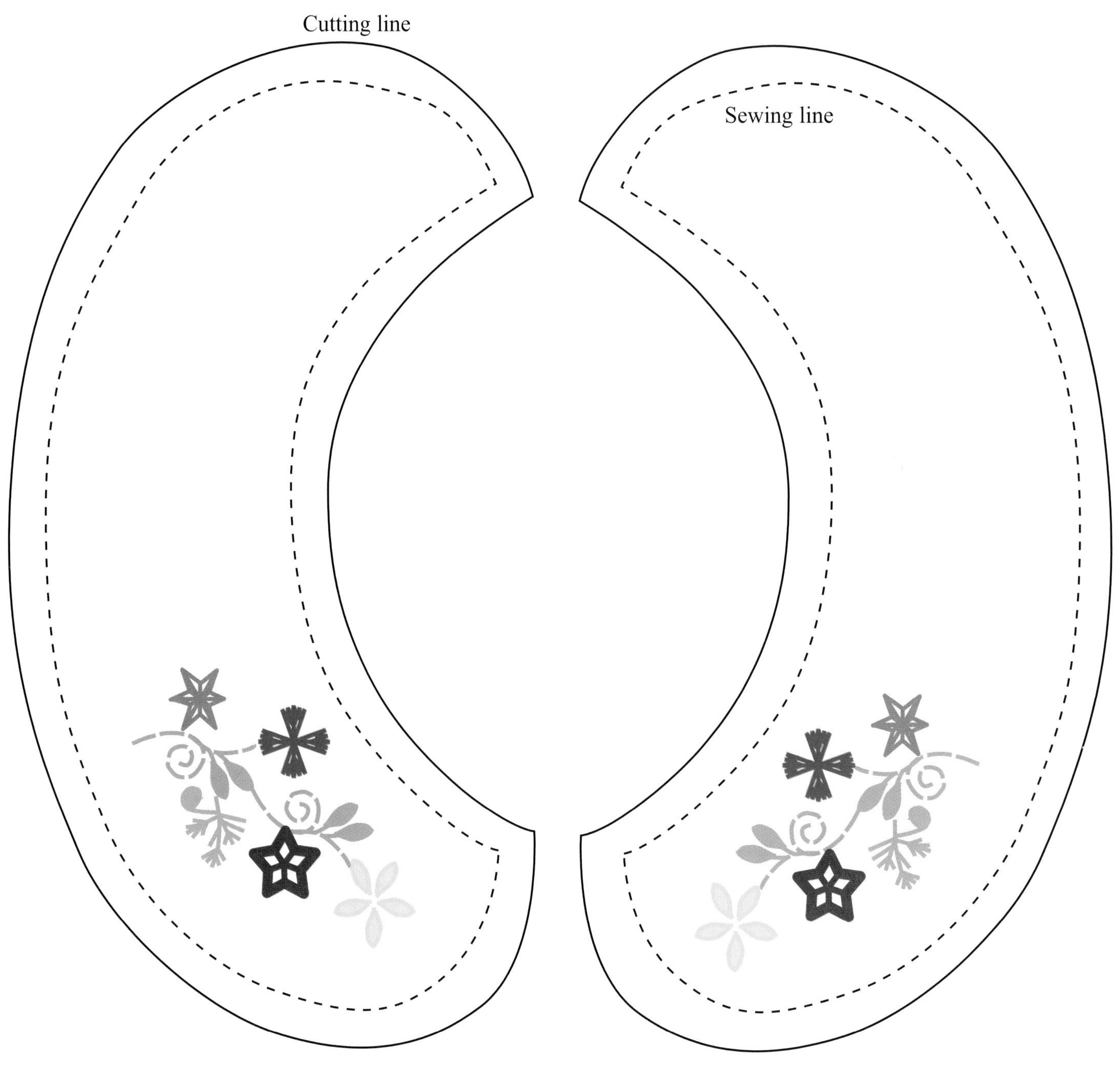
Cutting line
Sewing line

Quick Project

Little Girl's Purse

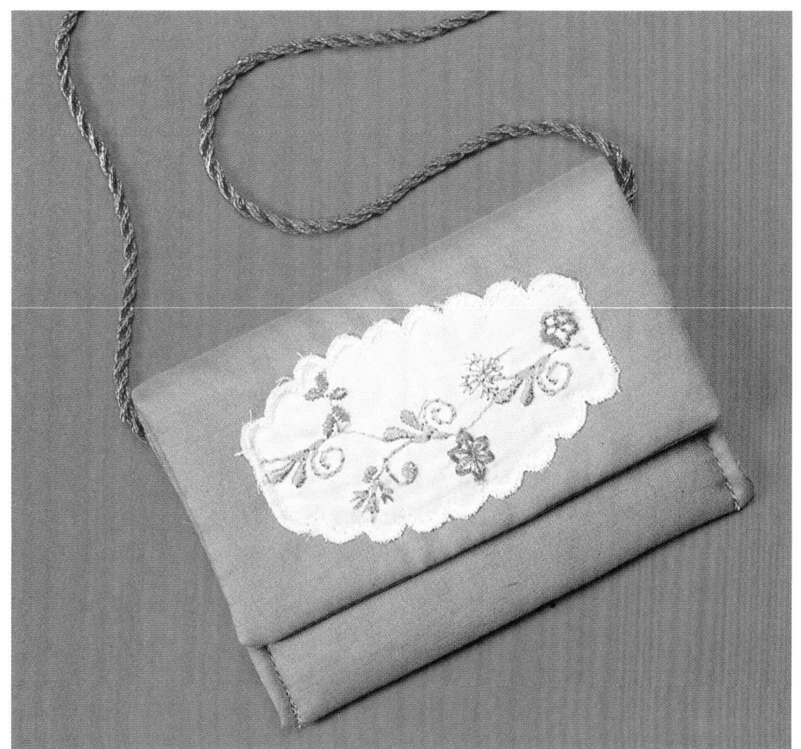

We had a 3" strip of embroidery left, with one messed up flower, but made into a little purse, it was the hit of the outfit.

Materials needed:

(2) Scraps of dress fabric 5" x 9"
Embroidered scrap
(1) scrap of fleece or batting 5" x 9"
2/3 yard of cord or ribbon for the strap

Thread to match fabric
(1) Velcro circle or square
Scrap of fusible web like Stitch Witchery

1. Following the diagram, sew the Velcro in place on the two pieces of fabric. Then sew the embroidery in place.

2. Place the two pieces right sides together on top of the piece of fleece. Stitch all four sides, using a 1/4" seam allowance and leaving a 2" hole to turn. Clip the corners and turn. Press and insert the scrap of fusible web in the turning hole. Press. Fold so the Velcro meets. Insert the cord or ribbon in the seam and stitch, forming the purse.

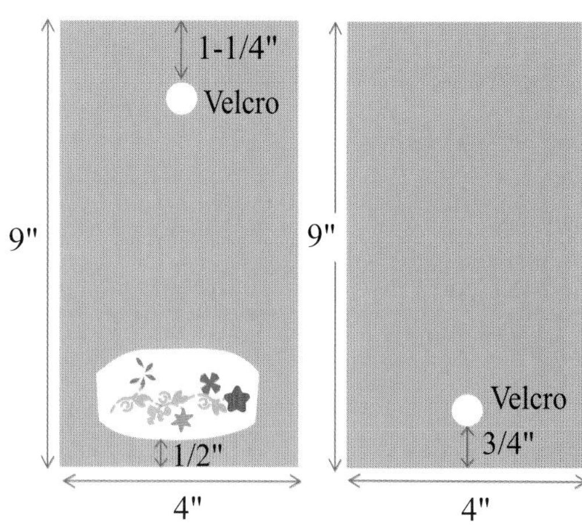

English Eyelet Embroidery

Called by a variety of names, Broderie Anglaise, Ayrshire, Madeira or Swiss work, this embroidery consists of open worked spaces, varying in shape and size, which are cut or punched with a stiletto and then overcast. The edges are traditionally finished in scallops. The classical period of eyelet work was the late 18th and early 19th century. It appeared on dress sleeves, caps, lingerie, baby clothes and linens. Originally, the embroidery consisted only of eyelets. Later, it was combined with additional embroidery similar to the Swiss embroidery. The traditional eyelet embroidery was worked as tone-on-tone embroidery. Some exceptions were Czechoslovakian embroidery worked in different colors.

For our eyelet work, we combined some of the traditional and some of the Czechoslovakian by doing a tone-on-tone and contrasting colors. We used the eyelet work and then other machine stitches combined to get the effect desired. This eyelet embroidery is one of the techniques you can do a lot or a little and each gives a very unique effect.

Embellished Blouse

Materials needed:

Lady's purchased blouse
Optional eyelet embroidery attachment (this attachment has several sizes of round punches included)
Stiletto or buttonhole punch
Matching or contrasting thread: blouse uses a light taupe silk thread, variegated green rayon

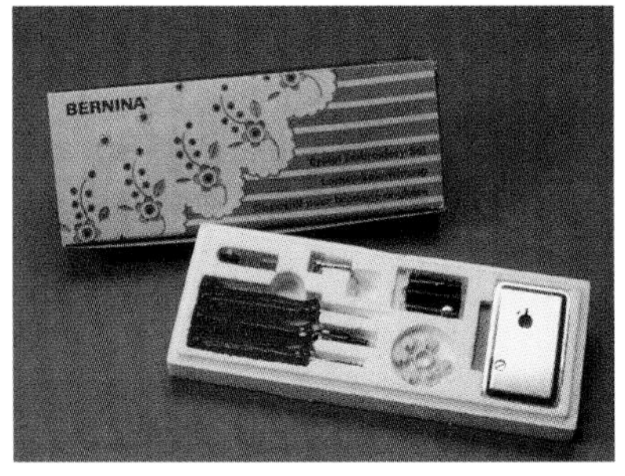

Directions will be given using the eyelet embroidery attachment, but would be the same if you were doing this "free hand." The only difference would be that you would have to carefully guide the stitches around the punched hole, and with the attachment, it does the guiding for you. Some of the newer machines have a circular straight stitch which could be used to "stay stitch" and then work the satin stitch around it. Many of today's computerized machines have the eyelet stitch built right in, just stitch and punch the hole afterward.

Punch holes with the punch for the larger holes, set machine:

Stitch selection: zig zag (1-3 depending on size of hole)
Stitch length: 0
Needle position: Half right (or so it comes barely into edge of hole on right swing)
Bring up lower thread
Lower feed dogs
Attach eyelet embroidery plate (if using)
Lower presser foot

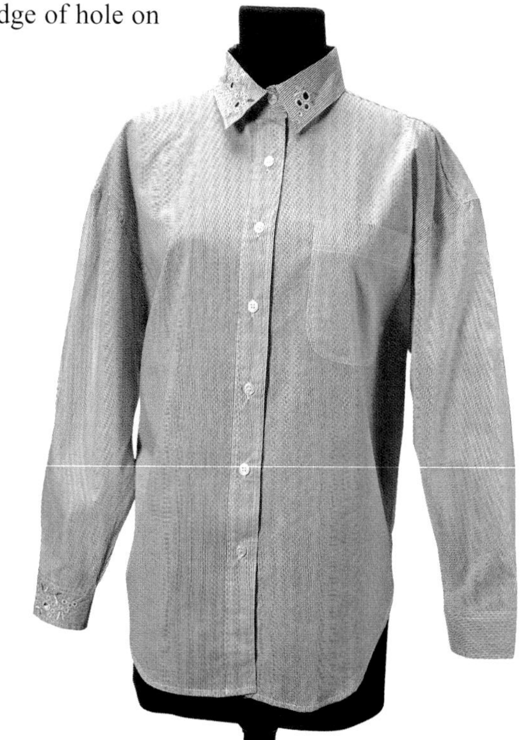

1. Transfer pattern to fabric. Practice on scraps to perfect the sewing techniques.

2. Sew around edge of hole once to secure, guide thread ends around pin, cut them off and adjust zig zag slightly wider. Stitch around a second time. To secure finishing threads, set stitch width to 0 and sew a couple securing stitches.

3. For large center holes, we used the 3/8" punch; for smaller surrounding petals, we used a stiletto to get a 1/8" hole to stitch around.

4. Stems were made using a 1-1/2 stitch width and a 1/2 stitch length.

5. Leaves were made setting machine to single pattern and working one petal stitch where desired.

A unique gift for a child is the lampshade we designed below, but if you use another design, this shade would be a very unique gift for a person of any age. It will update an old lamp or one that needs a replacement shade. If you have a good shade that the fabric is rotted on, you can remove it and reuse the frame. If you have a different shape frame, you will need to adjust the top shaping.

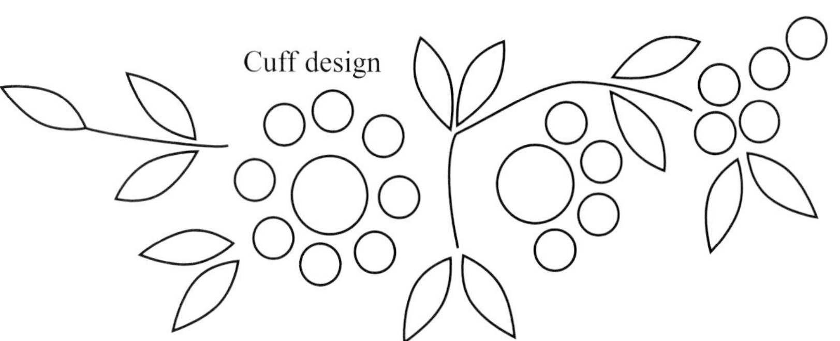

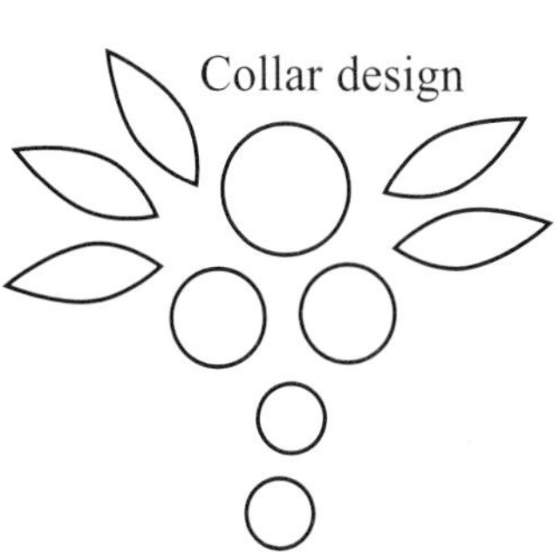

Quick Project

Lamp Shade

Materials needed:

Wire lamp shade (can be purchased at craft stores); ours had a 10" lower diameter
White cotton fabric 8" x 33"
Tan cotton thread
Green cotton thread
Red cotton thread
Bobbin thread
1/2" wide elastic (we used the clear)
Circular embroidery attachment as prior project used
Small embroidery scissors

1. Sketch or trace a cat design near center of fabric (so seam will end up in back). Position it about one inch from lower edge of fabric.

2. All holes on this project were made with stiletto to be 1/8" in diameter.

3. Stitch around holes as in step 1 above directions (for blouse).

4. When finished with tan cat outline, change thread and make green eyes.

5. With a triple straight stitch, sew the whiskers. Start from outside and work criss cross for the three whiskers.

6. Sew cat's mouth with a single scallop stitch and then another right above it in opposite direction.

7. Ears are a single satin stitch triangle in the tan thread.

8. Work scallop stitch, with green thread, along both edges of fabric and trim into scallops using a sharp embroidery scissors.

Now we are ready to assemble the shade:

1. Sew two 8" ends together. We made a French seam; you could also serge it.

2. Measure two pieces of elastic the diameter of the top portion of shade. Ours was 13".

3. On the shade frame we used, the elastic was attached 1/2" down and 1-3/8" below that. Attach elastic using a zig zag stitch set at 1 to 1-1/2.

4. Press, and place finished shade on frame, laying lower edge over lower edge of frame.

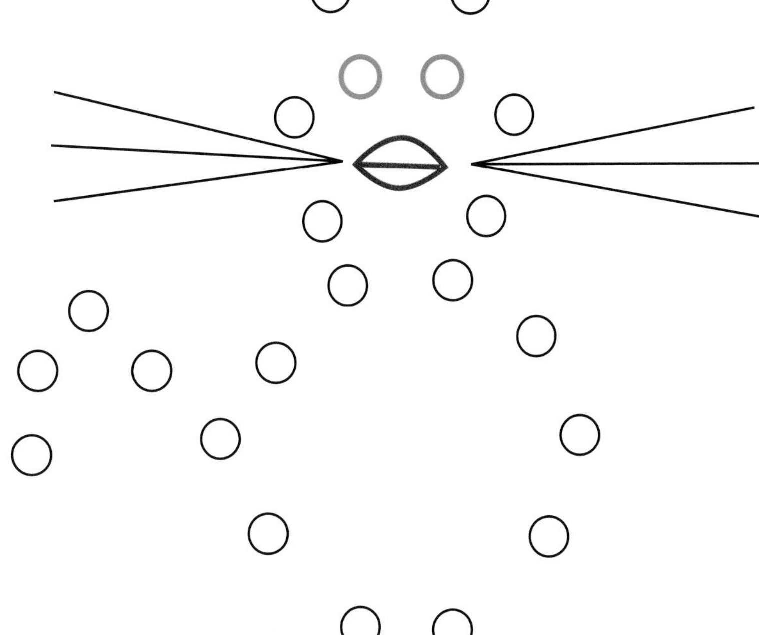

For most of the sewing machine accessories we mention in this book, your sewing machine dealer is the best place to purchase these items.

Depending on if the local sewing machine dealer/fabric store does not have what you need, try the following resources. If you do not see what you are looking for at a store, be certain to ask if they have or can get the item you need, be it a presser foot or stabilizer. Remember: there are no dumb questions.

Nancy's Notions
333 Beichl Ave.
P.O. Box 683
Beaver Dam, WI 53916
Customer service (920) 887-0391
E-mail nzieman@aol.com
Website http://www.nancysnotions.com

Clotilde, Inc.
B3000
Louisiana, MO 63353
Customer service: (800) 545-4002
Credit card orders: (800) 772-2891

Quilters' Resource, Inc.
P.O. Box 148850
Chicago, IL 60614
Customer service: (800) 676-6543
Fax: (800) 216-2374
Orders: (800) 676-6543

The following sources are for ideas only. They are all hand techniques and will not give any directions for machine techniques.

Vanishing American Needle Arts by Denise Longhurst, published by
G.P. Putnam's sons, New York

Antique Needlework, by Lanto Synge, published Blandford Press,
Poole/Dorset

The Romance of Lace by Mary Eirwen Jones, Spring Books; *London*

Brazilian Three-Dimensional Embroidery by Rosie Montague, Dover
Publications Inc., New York

The Art of Dimensional Embroidery by Marie A. Freitas, Published by the
Edmar Co., Camarillo, CA

Marie Duncan
E-mail: mmmgm@earthlink.net
Inquiries and questions

Betty Farrell
E-mail jjfarrell2@aol.com
Inquiries and questions

Bibliography

1. McNeill, Moyra. *Drawn Thread Embroidery*. Owl Book Henry Holt & Co., N.Y. 1989.

2. Microsoft ® Encarta. Copyright 1994 Microsoft Corporation. Copyright 1994 Funk & Wagnalls Corporation.

3. Silverstein, *Guide to Upright Stitches*. David McKay Co., N.Y. 1977.

4. Young, *Eleanor R. Crewel Embroidery*. Watts 1976.